Holding
Wholeness

(IN A CHALLENGING WORLD)

Holding Wholeness

(IN A CHALLENGING WORLD)

An Anthology By

DAVID SPANGLER

HOLDING WHOLENESS
(In a Challenging World)

Cover Art and Book Design by Jeremy Berg

Published by Lorian Press LLC
Holland, Michigan

ISBN: 978-1-939790-30-9

Spangler/David
Holding Wholeness (In a Challenging World)/David Spangler

First Edition August 2019

www.lorian.org

CONTENTS

INTRODUCTION 1

THE FIRST THREE STEPS 4

WHAT'S HAPPENING? 7

THE 3 C'S 10

BEING A GENERATIVE SOURCE 12

THE KNIGHT OF FIERY HOPE 15

ENERGY HYGIENE 18

BUILDING AN ENERGY HYGIENE FIRST AID KIT 24

SUBTLE ACTIVISM 42

VIEWS FROM THE BORDERLAND 49

A MESSAGE FROM A SUBTLE COLLEAGUE 69

TWO BLESSINGS 71

STANDING ACTIVISM 72

CONTINUING THE JOURNEY 75

A FINAL NOTE 76

ABOUT THE PUBLISHER 77

Holding Wholeness

INTRODUCTION

Wildfires, floods, rising sea levels, extreme heat waves, terrorism, mass shootings, political divisiveness and gridlock, trade wars, economic vulnerability, epidemics, cyberattacks: the world seems filled with threats and dangers, change and upheaval, conflict and violence, all amplified and broadcast through the immediacy of television, social media and the Internet.

Confronting all this on a purely physical level can be challenging enough, but we are not purely physical people, nor is the world a purely physical place. We all—people, animals, plants, landscapes—share a non-physical or subtle energetic dimension as well. On that level, the events in the world, both good and bad, exist as energetic patterns and waves that can have an impact as well, one that can directly influence our own subtle energetic, mental, emotional, and even physical well-being. This subtle impact can be greater because it is not constrained or lessened by distance. The gunning down of innocent worshippers in a mosque in New Zealand, for instance, sends energetic shockwaves throughout the collective energy field of humanity, which can be felt by sensitive individuals on the other side of the world. Further, the suggestive influence of such shockwaves can be picked up and embodied by individuals anywhere on earth who are predisposed to such violence and the ideas and emotions behind them. Resonance to these shockwaves can elicit compassionate acts from those attuned to compassion and the wellbeing of their community or, sadly, can elicit similar violent acts from those attuned to fear, hatred, and images of separation and conflict.

The bullets fired by a crazed gunman only travel a distance measured in feet; the hatred generated by that gunman's subtle energy field of thought and emotion can travel around the world.

So can the energies of love.

The reality of our time—of all times—is that we inhabit an energetic world ruled by principles of resonance, connectedness, and entanglement as well as a physical world ruled by the familiar principles of space and time. We know we have to deal with the latter; we have yet to fully learn that, to create a healthy and whole world, we have to deal with the former as well.

The good news is that we are far from helpless in this subtle dimension

1

of life. The same laws that allow one person or one group's hatred and fear to reach far beyond their geographical location and influence equally allow one person or one group's love and blessings to span the globe as well. And since the latter is more directly in harmony with the principles of coherency and wholeness—call them the principles of love—that underlie the subtle structure of the world, it can have a far greater and more long lasting impact than can the energies of hatred, no matter how it appears on the surface of things.

The fact is that each of us is like a power station of subtle energy; we are each a generative source, capable of contributing mightily to the wellbeing and evolution of the world. Learning how to stand in this identity and become powerful sources of wholeness is what Incarnational Spirituality is all about. It affirms our ability to live and act successfully in both domains of life, the physical and the subtle, working in partnership and symbiosis.

There are three elements to this, like the proverbial three-legged stool. The first is learning how to protect ourselves from the toxic and broken energies in the subtle environment. In Incarnational Spirituality, this is called "energy hygiene." The second is learning how to stand in our unique incarnate identity and generative power. We call this "Standing in Sovereignty and Self-Light." The third is learning how to connect with the world to be an active, positive, contributing force for wholeness, particularly within the subtle dimension. We call this "subtle activism" or "energy tending."

I've written a number of books dealing with all three of these elements of Incarnational Spirituality, but over the last ten years in particular, I've written smaller articles and essays addressing how we can deal with unwanted and distressful subtle energies and how we can add our own subtle energies in positive blessing to our world. Most of these have been written in response to questions asked in classes or through emails and letters from people asking what they can do to deal with what is happening in the world. People don't want to just be victims or suffer from despair and hopelessness; they want to make a difference. They want to be agents in birthing a better world.

The questions keep coming as, unfortunately, so do the disasters that prompt them. It seemed to me that it would serve a purpose to gather in one place all the various documents I've written in answer to these questions and the needs they pose. Hence, this anthology.

The articles and essays here cover a wide range of material; some assume some prior knowledge or familiarity with Incarnational Spirituality or with my work with the subtle worlds. At the end of this book, I've included some references to further sources where you can find more information, if you are interested. But I think the basic message and ideas presented here and their intent are clear. My hope is that you will find within them something that will be helpful, useful, and empowering for you.

The basic message is simple: the world is going through a difficult time, AND we have within ourselves the resources not only to survive but to thrive and make a positive difference. We *can* be effective and good subtle energy tenders in a challenging world.

THE FIRST THREE STEPS

When we feel the impact of negative subtle energies, there are three steps we can take immediately as our first response. These steps take the form of answering three questions:

What is my situation?
What are my resources?
What can I do?

The nature of subtle energies and of the subtle domain in which they propagate and manifest is that we can be impacted emotionally and mentally by forces that do not arise from anything or anyone in our immediate environment. There are chronic energies of anxiety and fear that percolate through humanity's subtle field much like smog through the air. We can all experience them no matter where we are, and we can all contribute to them, no matter what is happening. There are also "spikes" of negative subtle energy generated by a specific event somewhere in the world. It could be a mass shooting thousands of miles away, but the energetic impact of it could still hit us, amplified now by the way information is immediately shared around the world through social media and the Internet. It's not guaranteed we will feel such an impact, but distance is not a barrier to the subtle energies that carry it.

This means that if I suddenly feel fearful, angry, depressed, distressed, or threatened, my first step is to ask myself, "What is my immediate situation?" Is there a reason in my environment for me to feel these things? Is something happening around me that could cause an emotional or mental reaction. Is there a physical reality that I must deal with or is this a purely subtle response?

This was born home for me one day when I was feeling anxious for no particular reason. A subtle being, obviously responding to my feelings, appeared and asked me, "Is there something in your environment that is threatening you?" I was sitting in my living room at the time in a peaceful and quiet neighborhood. Nothing was threatening me, so I said, "No." "Then don't concentrate on the threat you feel but tune into the peace that is actually around you in your environment," my visitor said. (*I tell the whole story of this encounter in the except from my journal,* Views from

4

the Borderland, *that is included further on in this anthology.*)

Situational awareness—realizing that nothing was threatening me—allowed me to relax and center myself. It allowed me to attune to peacefulness, rather than becoming fixated on the energy of conflict and anxiety that I was feeling. Often, this is the most important thing we can do. Our tendency is to identify with and personalize subtle energies we experience because in many cases we experience them through our feelings. Taking stock of what is happening around us and actually being in the moment where we are can help us dis-identify from any resonance we are having with energies whose source is far away. We can say, "These feelings and the energy behind them don't originate with me; I need not identify with them."

This doesn't mean, though, that we can't respond. This brings us to the next question: "What are my resources?" What mental, emotional, and subtle energetic strengths and capacities do I have on which to draw? This doesn't mean having psychic abilities. It means having a mental and emotional core in which I feel strong, positive, centered, sovereign, and sacred. It means knowing myself as a generative source, not as a victim.

The secret to an effective response to subtle phenomena is to come from our core, just like a martial artist acts out from her core. But just as a martial artist needs training to do this well, so we need to develop and practice coming from a calm, balanced, centered core of identity and subtle energy—coming from what in Incarnational Spirituality is called our "Sovereignty." I need to know what resources of love, compassion, serenity, insight, balance, harmony, wisdom, and so on that I have to draw upon, based on my life experience and spiritual practice.

Incarnational Spirituality offers a tool-kit of principles and techniques for standing in our core Sovereignty and being our generative self, but so can other spiritual and psychological traditions and methodologies, at least those that do not denigrate our incarnate status or divide us between "higher" and "lower" parts of ourselves. Any tradition or methodology that enables us to experience our wholeness can give us resources for dealing with subtle energetic impacts. The key, though, is to practice in ways that build in a felt sense of our Sovereignty and wholeness, taking them out of the realm of ideas. Just as reading a book on aikido won't give us proficiency as a practitioner of this martial art, so reading about our sacredness or our inner core doesn't replace practicing these things in the midst of our daily lives.

Finally, once I have calmed myself through situational awareness and I know what my resources are, then I can ask, "What can I do?" Sometimes the answer is obvious. I may be inspired to energetically send love or blessing, peace or healing to a person or place. But just as first responders in the physical world have to assess what they can and can't do in a situation—that is to say, what actions will help and what actions might make things worse—so we don't want to just rush in to a subtle energetic situation of which we've become aware without asking just what contribution we can make that would be helpful.

I've learned this lessen more than once when, with the best of intentions, I've set about sending what I thought would be positive energies into a situation only to be told by my subtle colleagues to stop. Sometimes what is needed is to allow a situation to calm and settle down before we add new energies to it. Even positive energies can do harm if they simply add to an already overwhelming situation.

For instance, when the tsunami hit Japan and caused a potential meltdown in the nuclear power plant on the coast, I could feel the waves of distressed and fearful emotional energies coming through the subtle dimensions. I sat down to center myself, enter a peaceful center and then project that peace to that situation, believing that would help. I'd just started, though, when a subtle being appeared and asked me to stop. "Now is not the time," he said. "Conditions are energetically too turbulent. Wait. Your help will be welcome later."

Working energetically is a skill that can be developed like any other skill; often, many variables are involved. I have tried to describe some of this in my book, *Working with Subtle Energies*. But these first three steps are the basic responses whenever you feel impacted energetically. Ask these three questions, and you're on your way to being a calm, effective agent for wholeness in the energetic realms.

WHAT'S HAPPENING?

[As natural disasters and human catastrophes such as mass shootings and other tragedies continue to happen more and more frequently, I am often asked, "What is happening to the world? What is going on?" The following is excerpted from a letter I wrote to such an enquirer. It summarizes my best understanding of what is occurring now as seen from a subtle perspective.]

My understanding is that we're witnessing four things going on in the world: emergence, cleansing, resistance, and opportunism. Let me explain what I mean by each of these.

EMERGENCE: It's important to realize that a new world truly is taking incarnation around us. It is not always very visible yet, though elements of it are manifesting in individuals and groups around the world that are working on behalf of planetary wholeness. However, in the subtle dimensions, its energetic structure is present as a matrix around which new patterns can develop. As such, it is increasingly manifesting in the planetary subtle field. The subtle energetic environment is changing, affecting all levels of human and planetary life, acting as a source of inspiration and stimulation to bring ideas and actions into play that work for the good of the planet as a whole. In some cases, the subtle presence of this new world provides empowerment and relief to those who can attune to it or who are in resonance with it, but in for many people who are still attached to older ways of being, it's felt as a pressure to change and adapt, which is not always welcome and which can create anxiety.

This is not to say that the new world that is emerging is paradisaical or utopian; it's not "New Age" in the sense that people were expecting and projecting back in the Sixties and Seventies, a time in which everyone will be in a state of blissful and loving consciousness and oneness. The potential for this is there, certainly, but manifesting it will still take time and work. What will be different is that the effort to create states of wholeness and integration—to participate in the community of life—will be lessened. Wholeness on many levels will be easier to understand and achieve, but it still won't be automatic. The "instant planetary transformation" is and always has been a myth.

This change is on many levels: physical, emotional, mental, and subtle energetic. Some places will feel it more than others, just as rising seas will impact the coastlines of our country more quickly and significantly than they will the prairies of the Midwest or the mountains of the West. This means that the experience of change and of a new world emerging, and the ease and rapidity of that emergence in tangible forms, will not be uniform throughout the world.

CLEANSING: The second thing that is happening, cleansing, is a necessary component of this emergence.

There are neglected, buried, and broken human energies from our past that have never been resolved or healed. They cannot remain unobserved, unrecognized, and untreated as the new patterns emerge. This ancient material has to be brought out into the open, faced, and dealt with. An example of this is how racism in the US is now being brought more and more into the light to be dealt with. But all this stirring up generates unpleasant and anxiety-producing energies that we all feel and that can obscure the fact that good things are happening, too. If I'm renovating an old house that structurally is sound (as Gaia is) but that has asbestos in the insulation and mold in the wood, there's a lot I'm going to have to tear out that is no longer useful; for a time, there's going to be a lot of dust and disorganization and chaos as I remove what is rotten or harmful. If I step back, I can see the healthy, livable new house emerging. Still, living in the chaos of the renovation is not pleasant!

RESISTANCE. Organisms resist change. They particularly resist the arising of an environment in which they have to adapt, leave, or die. A lot of people are invested in some very ancient thought-forms and ways of being; this is far more than just a personality- or incarnate-level issue; it's a soul issue. There are those who will fight—and are fighting—tooth and nail to prevent changes and to maintain a status quo. They resist the cleansing and the emergence. A example of this in our physical world is the effort of white nationalists to fight the demographic changes in the US that will ultimately result in a more pluralistic society, one in which white men are one of several minorities and no longer a majority. This resistance can be tenacious, violent, and a cause of suffering, but it cannot win. The environment is changing. Still, we are in that in-between period when resistance is fierce and may likely grow more fierce, energetically

8

as well as outwardly. It's hard to give up old habits of thinking and feeling, especially when these habits are closely entwined with our sense of identity and power.

OPPORTUNISM. The current condition in the world is one of chaos being precipitated by the emergence of a new energetic system and the cleansing it both requires and promotes; where there is chaos, though, things become possible that might not have been possible before when everything was more structured. This cuts both ways. New possibilities of creating wholeness arise, and people can seize the opportunity to externalize these possibilities. By the same token, there are those who see in the chaos and fear of the moment an opportunity to seize power (not necessarily political) and advance their own agendas. This may be done in a good spirit, not out of malevolence or selfishness, but it can still complicate things because the vision behind such opportunistic activity may be limited and not responsive to the needs of a larger wholeness

In dealing with these four aspects of the world scene, it's important to remember that none of us is powerless. In our core, in our Light, in our soul presence and Sovereignty, we can stand in the unfolding energy of a new world right where we are and act out of that space. We can be the spirit and energy of this new, more collaborative, compassionate, inclusive, and integrated world. We each have the ability to be a loving and creative presence, an agent of wholeness, in our own daily encounters. Though this may seem a small thing, it is still a presence of power and it does make a difference.

THE 3 C'S

When it comes to dealing with subtle energies, we want to keep in mind the 3 C's: Core, Calm, and Connected.

All effective subtle work is anchored in and proceeds from our core, just as an effective martial artist acts out of her core or an athlete draws on his core strength. In Incarnational Spirituality, our core is our sacred identity manifesting as our incarnate Sovereignty, Self-Light, and generativity. It's like a radiant star. There are different ways of accessing this core, which we can experience as a felt sense of wholeness and coherency within us. In Incarnational Spirituality, we build this felt sense through exercises like Standing, Self-Light, the Presence Exercise, and the Inner Land Exercise, but any methodology that honors your incarnate identity and selfhood as an expression of sacredness can help you center in your energetic, incarnational, spiritual core.

From this core place, you fill your energy field, your thoughts, and your emotions with calmness. Imagine trying to thread a needle or drawing a straight line with a pen while your hands are shaking. The job is so much harder, and you may not be able to accomplish it. Similarly, if your own emotions and thoughts are agitated, your subtle energy field will be agitated, making it much harder to deal with subtle energies vibrating in your environment in agitating ways. If the world around you is energetically shaking, you want to be the calm center that quiets it down. Calmness gives you mastery and control over your own subtle energies in the moment, allowing you to work with confidence and carefulness.

Standing in your core and holding calmness within your field then allows you to connect to the energetic world around you, that is, to connect to the energy field of the things and people in the world around you. From calmness, you can connect in positive, loving, harmonious ways that spread that harmony outward into the subtle field of the planet. Further, you are entering into collaboration with all the other forces that are contributing wholeness and love to the world. Your own effectiveness is enhanced by this partnership, just as you enhance the effectiveness of others.

When we feel impacted by negative energies, our inclination is to withdraw, to pull back behind our boundaries and use our selfhood as a fortress protecting us from the world. At times this is necessary, but if overused as a technique, it can lead to isolation and alienation. In the subtle dimension as in the physical, sometimes the best defense is a good offensive. By radiating as a positive force, you are being active, not passive, and this can prevent negative energies from engaging with you. More importantly, unless you are connected to your world, your own gifts and positive energies are lessened in their ability to flow freely and with blessing into the world.

You don't want to connect out of need or fear or anger, which can happen when you act not out of your core or calmness but out of your reactive surface energies and agitation. Remember the 3 C's and step into your Core, hold Calmness, and then Connect the world with the loving and generative Soul that you are.

BEING A GENERATIVE SOURCE

In the midst of all the distressing and hurtful happenings in the world—not to mention the scale of some of the problems that confront us, such as climate change—it's easy to feel disempowered. What can you or I as single individuals do to make a difference?

Here are some helpful ways I have found to deal with this.

1. **Find Your Own Media.** Take the time and effort to seek out sources and stories of all the good that is happening in the world—and there is a lot of it! For from our time being plunged into a darkness of hopelessness, hope is being generated all over the place, often in small and local efforts to change the world and create wholeness but at times in large-scale efforts as well. The thing is that most national and Internet media are not geared to report on these kinds of things; they are attracted to the drama found in conflict and challenge, to the problems and not to the solutions. If you depend only on broadcast TV or news websites, not to mention the various partisan websites promoting adversarial positions and perspectives, you will not get a balanced picture of the world; chances are you will see little that can give you hope. But hope and vision and good works are all there to be found if you are willing to look for them.

I have found two good places to start on the Internet are Daily Good (dailygood.org) and Optimist Daily (optimistdaily.com).

2. **Joy Mining.** In the subtle worlds, joy is more than just a feeling of happiness. It is what I think of as a Heightening agent. When we can hold joy in our hearts and minds, letting it permeate our energy fields, it gets our energy moving and flowing in greater connection with the spiritual realms. But can we summon joy into and out of our energy fields when we want to? For many people, joy is a result of something good happening. Absent that good event, where does the joy come from?

I use a simple daily practice that I call "joy mining." Think of yourself as deliberately looking for "nuggets" of joy in your daily affairs and drawing them into your energy field, depositing them in an inner "bank account". To do this, you need to realize that joy doesn't have to be a dramatic experience of ecstasy and pleasure. It can be very simple. What you are looking for are moments that hold the potential of heightening you and your energy. Make a habit of noticing and acknowledging them so that you begin to realize that joy abounds and is all around us and within us for us to draw upon.

What might constitute of "nugget" of joy? It could be anything that in the moment gives you a warm, uplifted, open, happy feeling. It could be the pleasure of a good cup of coffee on a cold morning. It could be a smile from a friend. It could be seeing the blue of a clear sky or hearing the soothing sound of rain on the roof. It could be a song you hear, a funny remark, a bite of something delicious. Our senses are designed to connect us with pleasure in the world around us; when we acknowledge a moment of pleasure, we are in that moment sampling a joy nugget. It may not be the joy of winning a lottery of thousands of dollars or the joy of getting married, but it's a nugget of joy nonetheless. The more we acknowledge and collect them, the "warmer" our subtle energy becomes, a warmth we can then send out into the world around us.

The challenge is that we mentally establish a threshold of delight that has to be crossed before we will recognize the presence of joy. This is like saying that bits of gold dust are beneath my notice; all I'll mine are fist-size nuggets of gold. Yet as many a wealthy miner discovered, those little bits of gold dust can add up to a fortune.

The heart of Joy Mining is paying attention to moments of happiness, lightness, pleasure, and all-around OK-ness when they happen to you, even if they seem like small pleasures indeed. By paying attention, you are sensitizing yourself to this heightening energy. Further, it helps you realize that for you to pass on joy into the world, you don't have to be in a state of ecstatic happiness yourself. Though I can say from my own experience, as you practice this, the sense of being in the midst of joy gets progressively stronger until it can truly lead to moments of bliss and ecstasy in the midst of ordinary life.

This exercise is simplicity itself. The moment you feel pleased by something or have a sense of happiness about something you experience, pause for a moment and "collect" it. You do this by acknowledging the moment and honoring its felt sense within you. What is it felling like in your body? In your mind? In your heart? What subtle energy do you feel in this moment? Identify it to yourself by acknowledging, "This is a nugget of joy. In this moment, I am touching joy. Let it become part of me that I may radiate it onward in my life." Then give a silent thanks for the moment. Gratitude and joy go hand in hand.

Do this throughout a day and see what develops for you.

3. **Don't strive to make a difference in the world.** We all make a difference in our world just by being in it. This is no small thing. We have no way of measuring how a smile, a helpful word, a moment of appreciating someone else's effort or work, or an act of kindness may reverberate outward. This is especially true in the subtle world where distance is not factor but resonance can be. Any subtle energy I generate can affect any place or any person anywhere in the world if there is sufficient resonance or connection, which could be established through my clarity and strength of intention.

Paradoxically, though, if I strive to make a difference and base my sense of identity and self-worth on my ability to make a difference, then I can be setting myself up for both disappointment and disempowerment. I may feel that it's no use doing anything since anything I can do in my little corner of the world won't matter in the face of planetary problems. I feel dwarfed by scale. I can feel defeated before I even begin.

But scale is different in the subtle world. If I honor my generativity, my sacredness, my connectedness to the world, then "making a difference" will flow out from me. I work as effectively as I can within the opportunities and conditions that are open to me. But by standing in fiery hope, by standing in love and appreciation for the world, by standing in my sacredness and Sovereignty, by not giving up on the world but honoring my connections to it, I become a resource within the life of the planet.

For all the things I can't do, there are always things I can do, and if I do them with love, with joy, with honor for all around me, then the fruits of my doing will have consequences far beyond the apparent limitations of the physical realm.

The fact is we can and do make a difference, but the trick is to discover that we do so effortlessly not by striving or setting impossible goals for ourselves to measure our worth but by honoring ourselves and by giving the world the gift of who we are, however modest that may seem to us.

THE KNIGHT OF FIERY HOPE

[A central idea in the teachings of Incarnational Spirituality is that of "fiery hope." This concept is central in how we approach the world, no matter how hopeless or distressful things seem. It is an idea that was conveyed in a graphic way one afternoon when, as sometimes happens, a subtle being appears to offer a message or insight. This particular visitation occurred many years ago, but the idea of fiery hope continues to resonate through all that we do in Lorian and all that we offer. It is the spirit behind this anthology.]

A Visitation

I was sitting on a sofa in my home reading when a non-physical being abruptly appeared in the air in front of me. While this in itself was not unusual for me, the appearance of this being was. He looked like a knight out of a storybook, clad in shining golden armor, his face hidden within its helmet. On its chest burned a flame, as bright and radiant as a piece of sunlight. He said clearly, "I am a Knight of Fiery Hope! I speak to all humans. You are not entering a darkened age. You are entering a time when the Light of your creative spirit can manifest new vision and new life. Be what I am. Let fiery hope, not despair or fear, shape your world." Having delivered this message, this being then disappeared.

As always when dealing with subtle beings, the felt sense behind an encounter or communication is at least as important, and sometimes more so, than the actual images that are seen or the words that are used. The thought processes of such beings are invariably rich with interconnections and meanings, far more than can be accurately reproduced in a few lines of linear text. In this case, I was aware that what this being was saying had little to do with the future. He *wasn't* saying, "Have hope for the future" or "Have hope because everything's going to work out and your planetary problems will all be solved." Rather he was describing a creative presence and potential within us—something "fiery" in the sense of being active and dynamic and something that holds open the door of possibility.

The Nature of Hope

Hope does not depend on external or outer events. There certainly can be and are hopeful things happening in the world that are seeds of change, of goodwill, of compassion, of vision and creativity. But many of the events reported in all the various media that now bring news of the world into our lives are not hopeful and can lead people to feel hopeless and helpless.

No, hope doesn't arise from what's happening around us. It arises from us, from who we are, from what we can do and how we can engage the world. We are the creators of possibilities and potentials; we make the opportunities for something new and better to emerge in our world.

Hope that lives in an individual because that person has a powerful vision and understanding of his or her generative and sovereign nature is important. It's the kindling from which Fiery Hope takes flame. But the "fire" of Fiery Hope, that which enables it to be a force for change in the world, is fed by connection and relationship, partnership and collaboration. It is a flame rising out of what we do together as well as what we do as individuals.

A holistic vision of the world that includes acknowledgement of the subtle realms expands the possibilities of partnership to include not just other humans but the realms of nature as well, and it expands them to include not just physical beings but non-physical allies, too. It offers a scope for collaboration that is truly breath-taking. In so doing, it holds up the potential that the creative, life-changing, life-affirming "flame" of Fiery Hope can burn more brightly and more powerfully than we may have ever imagined before. We become participants in a world of Hope, bringing it into being, rather than victims in a world of hopelessness.

Fiery Hope

"Fiery hope" is an affirmation that we are a source of hope because we are—or can be—a source of change and new vision. A particular course of events may be inevitable, but our response to it is not. We can respond in ways we could not have predicted or that a simple description of the event would have predicted.

Hope isn't a wish; it's an inner capacity, first to be open to possibilities for action and vision that refuse to be circumscribed or defined by circumstances and which thus can be transformative in the moment, and second, to add our energy to bring those possibilities to life through action of some nature. It is "fiery" because it taps into our passion, our commitment, our intentionality, our spirit.

16

Hope *can* change the future by opening us to new possibilities and choices which can make a difference; but just as importantly, hope can change ourselves. It can change how we meet events that cannot in themselves be changed for one reason or another but which can be altered in their effects by how we respond, especially by how we work together and care for each other. Hope can make us resilient as well as creative. It is "fiery" because in honoring ourselves and what we are capable of doing both on our own and in conjunction with others, we can burn away hopelessness and the sense of helplessness that comes with it.

Those of us of a certain age will remember *Ecotopia,* a utopian novel published in 1975. It tells the story of a new country formed when Washington, Oregon, and northern California break away from the rest of the United States in order to create a nation founded on ecological principles and technologies. It was hugely influential in the burgeoning ecological and environmental movements of the time. When its author, Ernest Callenbach, died, he left behind a farewell letter. It discusses the many ecological challenges and other difficulties facing humanity. He then asks the question, "Although we may not be capable of changing history, how can we equip ourselves to survive it?" His answers include mutual support, teamwork, altruism, working on behalf of the common good, and the "enormously creative" power of collaborative thinking, all things I've discussed over the years in various writings. But the number one survival quality on his list is hope. Hope makes all the other things possible by opening us to them.

ENERGY HYGIENE

[In 2014, I wrote a booklet about Energy Hygiene as a complement to the Subtle Activism booklet Lorian had been sending to enquirers. The information is still pertinent and useful now.]

An Energy Ecology

We live in a world filled with energies of all kinds. Some are the electromagnetic forces that light our lights and heat our stoves and bring us voices over the radio and images on our televisions. But there are other energies that surround us as well, of which most of us are probably unaware but which can affect us just as powerfully. These are *subtle* forces generated by life, consciousness and spirit.

These forces are set into motion by things we do and feel and think, by our emotional and mental activity. There are subtle energies that radiate from our spiritual presence as well. At a physical level we experience these energies as the *chi* which martial artists use or the *prana* that is part of yoga.

These are meta-physical energies, and they are as much a part of our surroundings as the physical ones with which we are more familiar. They flow between people and between us and our environment. They form an energy ecology that can affect our feelings, our thoughts, and our overall well-being and vitality in both positive and negative ways.

Engaging with this ecology so that its effect on us and others is healthy, clear, life-giving, and positive is what **energy hygiene** is all about.

An Energy Body

Just as we have a physical body, we have an energy body as well. It receives impressions and vibrations from the surrounding energy ecology, and it radiates them out as well, reflecting the state of our own thinking and feeling. We are each a broadcasting and a receiving station combined.

Just as things you see and hear on the television can affect your emotions and your thoughts, so can these subtle energies as they engage with your energy body, though in a different way. We respond consciously to things we see and hear, but the energy body *resonates*

18

with the energies and impulses it encounters. It becomes like them, like a chameleon changing its skin color to blend with its surroundings. This resonance is unconscious for most people though the effects are not. We may feel our thoughts and feelings are our own and not realize we may have picked up some of them through the interaction of our energy body with the subtle energies in our environment.

"Damndruff" or Psychic Lint

Generally speaking, our energy body has its equivalent to our physical immune system and resists intrusion. But through resonance, it can pick up bits of subtle energies in much the way a sweater picks up lint. Depending on the nature of this "psychic lint" (which I sometimes call "damndruff") and the resonance it has with us, it can cling and influence us with its qualities and energy. Usually, it's a bit of mental or emotional information, saying "feel this emotion" or "think this thought." For example, if you go into a room filled with anxiety, you may not know consciously what has happened but your energy body senses and picks up the anxious energy in the room. Bits of "anxiety lint" attach, giving you the message, "Feel fear. Feel anxious." And this energy message, like any other stimulus from the environment, can pass into your unconscious mind and then into your consciousness. You find yourself feeling anxious but for no reason that you can detect.

We are all shedding such psychic lint and damndruff into our environment all the time from our thoughts and feelings. Most of it dissipates and is transformed, but some of it persists and builds up, accumulating in certain places or around a person. It can be positive or negative in its effect. The home of a spiritual person can radiate with uplifting subtle energies, making us feel good the moment we cross the threshold. But the home of someone in the grips of depression may be filled with depressive thoughts and feelings that give the atmosphere of the place a gloomy feel even if the owner is not present.

In the normal course of our day, we may pick up and discard such lint many times. But sometimes it is not discarded. We carry it with us and it can begin to accumulate. Bits of subtle energy become stuck within our own energy body. When this happens, such a stuck place can become a "lint trap" attracting and holding to other bits of psychic lint that we may encounter. Energy hygiene is a way of clearing this stuff away and removing it so no one is affected adversely by it.

Energy Connections

In the physical world, we are separated by distance. What happens to someone on the far side of the earth may seem to have little consequence or affect upon me. We believe our thoughts and feelings are private, locked within our skulls and our skins. But in the energy world, we are all connected in profound and interdependent ways. It's as if we were all standing on a great trampoline. When one person bounces, it makes the whole trampoline move and we all bounce to some degree. Subtle energies are not limited by distance. Thus when a calamity strikes in some part of the world, our energy bodies all feel the effect of the suffering and fear no matter where we are. We may feel uneasy or restless, anxious or fearful for no reason we can see.

We live in turbulent, troubling times. The news is filled with one crisis after another from war and terrorism to economic turmoil to global climate change. People are afraid, and this fear is often intensified by public media. Through our technological ability to communicate images, thoughts, and feelings quickly and dramatically, we have developed ways of blowing our psychic lint—particularly our fears, anxieties, angers, hatreds, and pessimism—around the world so that it affects all of us. Where in previous centuries, such subtle psychic lint would have dissipated and transformed, now it is repeated, reinforced, and strengthened by global media and our subtle energy connections until it accumulates in our world, no longer just "lint" but true psychic pollution weighing upon all of us.

Energy Hygiene

Energy hygiene is a procedure for dealing with psychic lint and psychic pollution. It is a way of working with subtle energies to create a clear, clean, positive, vibrant and healthy energy environment both within ourselves and in our immediate environment. When we use these procedures to deal with larger issues of psychic pollution in the world, then it becomes energy activism, which is simply energy hygiene for the planet at large.

More Than Protection

Good physical hygiene is about more than taking a shower or keeping clean; it's about all that we do to ensure the health and optimal function of our body. The same is true with energy hygiene. There are techniques of "lint removal" that can be learned and also ways of protecting ourselves to keep the psychic lint off in the first place. But energy hygiene is much more than just a defensive or cleansing process. It's about vitalizing and expressing a healthy wholeness of spirit, mind, heart, and body. It's about honoring and nourishing sovereignty, identity, coherency, and boundaries on the one hand and developing and practicing connectedness, engagement, love, and a compassionate participation in life on the other. Energy hygiene is the expression of an incarnational spirituality. *SAYS it All*

Three Rules

There are three rules of good energy hygiene.

Flow
Positivity
Connectedness

Each of us is like a pool of energy. As long as energy is flowing in and out in a healthy way, this pool is alive, clear and clean; when this flow is obstructed by a buildup of psychic lint, then the pool can begin to stagnate. Restoring and maintaining a healthy flow of energy is important. A good walk, physical activity, learning something new, doing something kind for someone else are all simple ways of restoring flow; there are also techniques for restoring this flow on a subtle energy level. The exercise included here is one example of such a technique.

Being positive is more than just practicing positive thinking, though that can be helpful. Positivity is a condition of being radiant, open, giving, confident, and strong. It is an energy state as much as a psychological one. There are many ways of developing and maintaining this state, but they are all enhanced by valuing and honoring yourself and standing in your uniqueness and sovereignty.

Connectedness opens us to a larger world beyond ourselves and enables us to participate in a greater wholeness. Just as a pool stagnates that is unconnected to living streams of water and ultimately to the ocean on the one hand and the wellsprings deep within the earth on the other, so we need to be connected to the vitality and life, the spirit and wellbeing of the world around us. We create good energy conditions for ourselves not by isolating ourselves behind shields and barriers but by creating good energy in the world around us. Compassionately and lovingly participating in the life of our world and contributing to the wellbeing of all life is a vital part of energy hygiene.

An Exercise

This is an energy hygiene exercise for dealing with fearful energies. A consequence of feeling fearful subtle energies is constriction, the "deer in the headlights" syndrome. We freeze. Our energies seize up. Flow is diminished. We lose connection to the universe.

Here is a very simple exercise to get flow going again:

1. Make a Connection: Reach out and touch something. Feel its texture and nature under your fingers. Let your attention flow towards the object you're touching. Appreciate it for what it is.

2. Expand your Heart: Think of a happy memory or pleasurable moment, something that gives you an inner sense of expansion, and draw that memory into your heart where you can feel it as a warm glow within you. Allow this glow to expand. Positive feelings create openness and receptivity in yourself and in the world around you.

3. Send Love through your Connection: Direct the feeling of this expanding glow out from your heart, down your arm and into your fingers and into the object you're touching. Feel love develop for the object you're touching. Pause to appreciate the relationship and flow you have with this object.

4. Connect to Cosmos: Be aware that you are standing within a vast, living world, one filled with abundant, flowing energy and love. Let the feeling of spaciousness surround you and fill you. Imagine the whole cosmos embraced and held by a loving presence. Feel the love of this

presence flowing into your expanded, glowing heart and down your arm and your hand and your fingers into the object you are touching. Feel yourself and this object expanding as this spaciousness flows into and around you.

5. Connect to Environment: Let this flow of spacious energy and love flowing from the cosmos through your heart and into the object you're touching now flow out from that object into the environment around you. As it does so, you find yourself and your energy field bathed and participating in a flow of energy from the cosmos and the sacredness within it through you and around you into and through the object you're touching and into the environment.

6. Complete the Circuit: See the flow of spacious, loving energy rising from your environment back into the cosmos, back into the sacred, completing the circuit. Just feel the energy of this flow moving through and around you, bathing you, bathing your environment; it's a current flowing from the sacred into you, through you, out from you and into the environment through the object you're touching, and back into the sacred.

7. Hold your Energy: As you stand in this flowing circuit, hold yourself and your energy field, along with whatever fears, negativity, or stuckness you were experiencing, in this flow, like holding dirty clothes under a rushing stream. You don't have to do anything except release your energy field to be filled, cleared, cleansed, and blessed.

8. Moving On. When you feel complete, let go of the object you were touching, breaking the circuit. Invite and allow the sense of connection to a larger, more spacious whole and the sense of your own energy flowing and circulating to integrate gracefully into your body and into your life. Express your gratitude to all involved and to the world around you. Your flow restored, go about your daily activities.

BUILDING AN ENERGY HYGIENE
FIRST AID KIT

[In 2009 for one of my online Lorian classes on working with subtle energies, I compiled an "Energy Hygiene First Aid Kit" as a way of helping students think about ways of constructively dealing with the subtle energies they were encountering in the world around them. Ten years later, I revised it for a similar class. I offer this revised version here.]

In a first aid kit, you find compartments with various things you may need: bandages in one compartment, disinfectants in another, and so on. I'm using this same image to present some suggestions for energy hygiene when you feel yourself in an emergency or when you need energetic cleansing.

COMPARTMENT ONE: IDENTITY

Overview: When we think of energy hygiene, what often comes to mind are issues of psychic protection, shielding, dealing with negative energies, and the like. But the function of energy hygiene is to preserve and maintain the integrity and wholeness of our identity as manifested through our energy fields, just as the function of our body's immune system and natural healing capacities is to maintain and preserve the integrity and identity of our body. When we talk about negative energies or protecting ourselves from intrusive psychic forces, what we usually are referring to are forces that in some manner make us less than we are (or can become) or diminish the integrity and wholeness of our overall beingness.

Think of "identity" here as an organizing principle, that which gives you coherency and makes you "you." Metaphorically, it's like the operating system of a computer which organizes all the computers functions and tells the software what to do. A virus or "bug" in the computer compromises that operating system and at times co-ops it, getting it to do other things, like sending unwanted messages out to your entire email list without your knowledge.

Like fish, we move throughout our day in a sea of energies made up of intentions, ideas, thought-forms, images, wishes, desires, impulses—all the stuff that human beings radiate through the activity of our minds and feelings. Much of this never leaves our own energy fields, but some of it does and becomes part of our common environment, just as our bodies emit chemicals, we shed bacteria, and viruses spread between us. And like viruses, these energy bits can snag us and then use our living energy system to sustain themselves or to continue whatever vector of purpose or desire lies behind their creation. Thus, a fad can spread amongst a group of people as the energy behind a particular idea or fashion or behavior is picked up and passed on just like we might spread the virus of a cold. In fact, although this is a metaphysical idea, the world of science has picked up on this and given a specific name to such "energy bits" that move between us. They are called "memes," the mental and emotional equivalent of a gene, and are thought of as units of cultural reproduction, the means by which ideas and intentions spread throughout a culture. They are sometimes also called "viruses of the mind."

For instance, a person who's happy can "infect" others with the energy of his or her happiness, and a person who's "down" and sad can pass the energy of those feelings on as well. If I pick up those energy bits, I may feel happy or sad (depending on their "vector" or character), but these emotions do not originate with me and are not really my own. I may only feel them for a moment and then shrug them off, or they may stay with me through the day.

We cannot avoid these energy bits, and we are sending them out ourselves. They are just a part of our environment like dust or bacteria. They can be helpful and good or distressing and negative. Most of them are probably irrelevant to our lives. The main point is that most of them are not very strong or long-lasting at all. If they attach to us, they do so usually because of resonance (they find something familiar or "friendly" and accepting in our energy fields) or because of proximity.

The fastest and best way to clear ourselves of such unwanted energy bits is to stand in the energy and light of our own identity. If they are not part of us, they burn or fall away or become absorbed into our field and assimilated ("resistance is futile!") Indeed, having a clear sense of our own individuality and identity and of our connections to life, the world, the sacred, the soul, and a clear felt sense of our incarnational field is absolutely the best defense and cleansing technique for the majority of energy phenomena that we may run into. Think of it this way. These little energy bits are like tiny voices saying "Do this, do that, go here, go there" but our identity is a huge voice saying loudly "This is who I am and this is what I'm going to do, this is where I'm going to go," and so on. The tiny voices have no chance against the loud, clear one, and shut up.

1. **The Standing and Self-Light exercises**. These are two core exercises within Incarnational Spirituality. They are valuable ways of attuning to and feeling the spirit of your sovereignty and identity. Doing these exercises can be an act of energy hygiene.

STANDING EXERCISE

As you do this exercise and move up the different levels from the physical to the spiritual, be aware of an axis of power, energy and identity rising up within you, connecting all these levels together. Like an inner spine, this is your Sovereignty. It is the core of your soul's identity emerging through you and as you. It is your sacredness. What you are looking for is the *felt sense* of this energy and identity within you.

<u>Physical:</u>

The physical action of this exercise is simple. From a sitting position, you simply stand up. Be aware of the physical sensation and felt sense of standing. Feel the work of your body, the power of balance that keeps you upright. If you are already standing, become aware that you are standing and be mindful of the felt sense of standing. In standing you are asserting your physical power to rise up against the power of gravity that would pull you down. You are celebrating your strength. If you are physically unable to stand, you can still assume an inner attitude of standing, perhaps simply by straightening your spine as much as possible.

<u>Emotional:</u>

Feel the power of being upright. Feel how standing singles you out and expresses your individuality and sovereignty. You stand for what you believe, you stand up to be counted. Standing proclaims that you are here. Standing says you are ready to make choices and decisions. Feel the strength and presence of your identity and sovereignty.

Mental:

Celebrate your humanness. You are an upright being. You emerge from the mass of nature, from the vegetative and animal states into a realm of thinking and imagining. In standing, your hands are released from providing locomotion. Feel the freedom of your hands that don't have to support you but can now be used to create, manipulate, touch, and express your thoughts, your imagination, and your sovereignty.

Energetic (Magical):

When you stand, your spine becomes a magical staff, the axis mundi and center of your personal world, generating the field that embraces you. The spine *is* the traditional wizard's staff along which spiritual power flows and the centers of energy sing in resonance with the cosmos. Feel your energy field coming into alignment with the stars above, the earth below, and the environment around you. Feel your energy aligning with the sovereignty of all beings above, below, and around.

Spiritual:

Standing, you are the incarnate link between heaven and earth. Your energy rises into the sky and descends into the earth. Light descends and ascends, swirling along your spine in a marriage of matter and spirit. This energy is both personal and transpersonal, giving birth to something new, something human, individual and unique. Feel the magic and energy of your sovereignty that connects soul to person, the higher-order consciousness with the consciousness of the incarnate realms. Feel the will that emerges from this connection, the spiritual presence that blends heaven and earth, aligning with the Sovereignty of creation as it manifests through you.

In doing this exercise of Standing, physically stand if you are able. If you are not able to do so, then be as upright as you can be in your physical situation and in your imagination, "stand" mentally and emotionally. The important thing is to have the felt sense of standing and being upright even if you are physically unable to do so. As you do so, work through these levels of sensation, feeling, thought, energy, and spirit, appreciating the power, the freedom, and the presence emerging within you from the simple act of standing. All of these manifest your unique Sovereignty, connecting and aligning you with all levels of your being, providing an axis around which integration and coherency can occur, creating wholeness and establishing your capacity for agency and self-governance.

SELF-LIGHT EXERCISE

Imagine a spiritual star at the center of the earth. It's a green star radiant with the power of planetary life. Imagine the light from this star rising up through the earth, surrounding you, bathing and nurturing the cells of your body and forming a chalice around you.

Imagine a spiritual star within the sun in the sky. It's a golden star radiant with the power of cosmic life. Imagine the light from this star descending from the heavens and pouring into the chalice of earthlight that surrounds you and fills your cells.

Where the green and golden lights of these two stars meet in you, a new star emerges, a radiant star of Self-Light, born of the blending of the individual and the universal, the planetary and the cosmic, the physical and the spiritual, Soul and Earth. Here two great forces, Cosmos and Earth, are blended by the love and will of the Soul acting at the heart of your incarnation.

This Self-Light is constantly being generated by the deep processes of your incarnation. You can obscure it but you cannot extinguish it. It surrounds you and fills you, always there for you to recognize and acknowledge, attune to and enhance with your attention and intention to let it shine upon the earth. You are a radiant, generative Source of Self-Light within a pillar of spiritual energy rising from the earth and Gaia and descending from the cosmos and Soul.

Take a moment to feel the generative star of this Self-Light within and around you. It is your connection to the earth, your connection to the cosmos, your connection to your own unique and radiant Self. Take a deep breath, drawing this Light into and throughout your body; breathe out, sending this Light out into your world. Filled with this Light of Self, attuned to heaven and earth, go about your day as a star of blessing.

2. **Build a positive image of yourself.** This image should be built around the core of a felt sense of what you love in your life and about yourself. Make a list of a series of statements about your life and the things and people in it, where each statement has the following sense to it: "I love that [whatever or whoever it is] is in my life; I enjoy and celebrate myself and my life because [whatever or whoever it is] is part of it. This list should give you reasons for celebrating who you are in positive ways.

3. **Build an "identity talisman."** This is something that holds for you the positive energy of your identity and which when you see it or hold it conveys that positive energy to you. For example, many indigenous shaman carry "medicine" or "mana" pouches that contain various items considered to have spiritual or magical energy. An "identity pouch" would contain small items that are uniquely meaningful to you in conveying the magic and spirit of your own life. I have such a pouch which is small enough that I could wear it under my shirt around my neck. It contains things, usually bits of stone or soil or plants, from all the most significant places in my life. This pouch contains the energy of my autobiography and puts me in touch with the energy of those places that have had a positive impact upon who I am. If I'm feeling pressured or beleaguered by subtle energies in my life, I can hold my pouch and tune in to the flowing energy of my identity which helps to re-center me and give me equilibrium.

4. **Do some loving act towards yourself.** Love is a most powerful force in energy hygiene, and when you show love towards yourself, it can be very healing, cleansing, and an act that gets your energies flowing again in positive ways. You want to feel good about who you are.

5. **Create an Appreciation Timeline**. This is a timeline or record of your life that marks your accomplishments, your growth points, your changes, the important events, wisdoms gained, and so on. Sometimes in the midst of living, we forget just what a rich current of energy, life and experience our incarnation embodies. It can be good to remind ourselves of that. Even the bad bits where we've been wounded or hurt can contribute wisdom and insight—or at least a sense of compassion for others feeling the same wounds—to our wholeness. Creating this time line is an exercise (and it could take an artistic form, like a collage of images and words), but once you've done it, it is there to inspire you and give you perspective when you may need it.

6. **Take an "Identity energy shower."** Just as you take a shower or bath to clean away the dirt you pick up as you go through your day. Attune to the felt sense of your incarnational field. Imagine this field as a ball of light above your head. Feel and imagine this ball swelling into a sphere and then this sphere descending over you. It passes over your head, over your shoulders, down over your torso and arms, over your hips and your legs and down over your feet until you are entirely encompassed within this sphere of light. As this sphere passes down over you, it pushes away or transmutes any unwanted or unneeded energy bits, influences, thoughts, feelings, and so forth that you may have picked up through the day. Do this as many times as feels good and comfortable to you. You can even do this while taking a physical shower. If so, draw as well upon the cleansing energy of the element of water. Feel this cleansing energy pass through your energy field as well, cleaning away unneeded and unwanted bits.

7. **Call on your "star power."** Using the Self-Light exercise, stand in your self-light and your incarnational field. Feel their power within and around you like a radiant sun. At the heart of your identity, is a core of love and intentionality that is part of your soul; your self-light and your incarnational field emerge from and embody the Light and power of this core. Feel this core expand, intensifying the light within you and completely filling your body and your incarnational field. Feel this core expand to fill the operational energy field around you. See yourself as a blazing star, a radiant sun, radiating the light of your presence, your love,

your sovereignty and sacredness. Anything that is not part of this light, anything that cannot harmonize or integrate with it or serve it in some manner cannot stay. Hold this radiance for as long as feels comfortable or appropriate, then let it sink down into the core within you, leaving your energy field transparent and vibrant and clear, resonating in harmony with your core identity.

These are just some suggestions. Anything that attunes you to the light and power and spiritual presence of your unique identity is going to have a positive effect upon your energy as a whole. Experiment and see what works for you and what "first aid" techniques you come up with.

COMPARTMENT TWO: LIFESTYLE

Overview: By lifestyle, I mean things like diet, exercise, one's routines and rhythms, habits, and so forth. A lifestyle is a very personal thing. It's quite true that what works for one person will not for another. What is at issue here is how your lifestyle affects your energy overall. How does it give you energy? How does it take it away? This is an assessment only you can make. However, there are some general principles I've found to be true, and I have a couple of suggestions for techniques that can be helpful.

1. **General good health principles.** These include good diet, keeping fit, having exercise, and getting enough rest and sleep, all of which absolutely have an effect upon our overall subtle energy field. Some of this effect is direct and some of it comes from the physical body's ability to hold energy, something that is harder to do if you're physically depleted or tired. The paradox is that while the subtle energies we're talking about here are non-physical, engaging with them is work which does take physical energy.

2. **An Energy Walk.** One technique that works well for me in balancing out and cleansing my operational energy field is to take a walk. Not only is this good exercise which in itself, by helping my physical energy, helps my overall energy system, but it has the added benefit of setting energy in motion (the flow principle again). And depending on where I walk, I can get a good "scrubbing" from the energies around me.

31

In this instance, the best environment for an energy walk is out in nature. This is not absolutely required, as anything that gets me out in the fresh air and sunshine is going to expose me to fresh, clean energies generally speaking. But when I walk in an area where there are plants and trees, I move through their living, vital energy fields which can impart vitality to my own.

Furthermore, most of the "energy bits" I get stuck to me during a day are like lint. Unless I'm holding on to them for some reason or creating a hospitable environment (for instance, my sadness creates an environment that can pick up and hold on to the sadness energies from others), they are all on the surface of my energy field. When we move through nature and through overlapping energy fields from the life around us, this stuff gets "brushed" off. In a way, we can do this for each other, too, which can be a real service, but this takes attentiveness to what we're doing. I'll talk about that in the Class Text Three material.

If going out into a natural environment, such as a wood or a park or wilderness area, is not possible or convenient where you live, then an energy walk can take place just as well in a city or suburb, but it requires some attention. In this case, you want to imagine yourself moving through the field of sunshine or through the energy of the air or rain, or simply through the energy field of the earth beneath your feet. In short, draw on the elements around you and their energy to "brush you off" and cleanse your energy field.

3. **Create an energy date with yourself.** This is taking time just for yourself in the midst of your lifestyle. Quite apart from what you do in this time—read a book, go to a movie, have a cup of coffee or tea at your favorite hangout place, visit with a friend, and so on—the fact that you are intentionally doing something just for yourself in a spirit of appreciation and love for who you are is an energy boost and can be restorative.

4. **Learn and stretch.** One of the best ways to get stuck energy moving again or to enhance the flow of your energy is to push past your boundaries and habits and do something new. Learn something new. Stretch your sense of what you are capable of. Expand your knowledge.

5. **A Habit Map.** Take some time to "map" or list all the habits of

action, mind and feeling you can think of. Be a naturalist in your own life and seek out and observe your habits and repetitive reactions, where they occur (their habitat), what they do (their behavior), and how they affect you. You want to get a sense of how much you are a creature of habit, or how much habits "in-habit" you (and "in-hibit" something new from emerging in your lifestyle). You are not judging these habits at first, you just want to list them and make a map of how much of your life is shaped by habitual behavior and what that shape may be. Many habits are good ones and are there for a reason to make our life simpler, but some habits are not so good or are outworn and no longer useful.

I'm not talking only about habits of action but also habits of thought and feeling. The principle is that our energy flows and sparkles most where we are mindful and fresh in what we are doing; when we go on automatic pilot and in effect doze off while engaging with life, our energy pulls back and goes into minimal mode. This doesn't mean that the actual expression of energy in the moment may not be intense. If I have a habit of always getting passionately angry when thinking of certain politicians, the energy I feel may be hot and volatile, but it's still a "dead" energy in that it's not coming from actual thought and mindfulness in the moment. It's zombie energy, lurching out of my past for whatever reason, long past the time when it should have been decently buried and allowed to decompose! The purpose of a habit map is to see those areas in your life where mindfulness, beginner's mind, fresh approaches, new insights, and greater awareness may pay rich rewards of energy, as well as those areas where your habits are serving you well and should be left alone.

COMPARTMENT THREE:
ATTITUDES, BELIEFS, THOUGHT-FORMS

Overview: Our thoughts and feelings, attitudes and beliefs about ourselves can all affect how we experience our own energy, as well as how that energy flows and patterns itself within and around us. Being aware of our emotional and mental state is an important part of good energy hygiene. The surface layer of our operational subtle field—our energy "skin"—can respond very quickly to our thoughts and feelings, while over time the deeper levels of that field reflect our habitual mental and emotional states.

1. **Happy Thoughts**. The idea of being a "Pollyanna" is frowned upon by many; being a "love and light-er" is a term of derision and contempt in some circles. But the fact remains that the body and its energy field respond to happy thoughts or more precisely to the felt sense of openness, wonder, and flow that such thoughts can induce. It isn't just any happy thoughts, either, but images that are unique to you and that give you a sense of well-being, safety, wonder, openness, and joy. As William Bloom points out in his excellent book, *The Endorphin Effect*, such thoughts release endorphins, neurochemicals that enhance the wellbeing and health of the body. The technique is to ask yourself what in your life gives you a sense of joy, peace, calm, togetherness, wholeness and so forth. For many people, it is very simple thoughts or images: a favorite place, a pet, a memory of a happy day, thinking of a loved one, and so forth. For me, it's thinking about my wife and kids. To restore a sense of energy flow and lightness in the moment, give yourself a "happy thought vacation" and take a moment to focus fully upon those images or memories that work for you. Close your eyes and just bask in the pleasure of that image or memory and let good feeling and good will flow through you. Reassure yourself that you're not escaping from the world by doing this but rather giving yourself a quick recharge of your energy batteries so, if need be, you can reenter the fray of daily life reenergized and quickened.

2. **Beliefs about yourself**. Another large influence on the state of your subtle energies is your attitude or belief about yourself. By this I don't mean philosophical, political, religious, or economic beliefs. Your body and your energy field neither know nor care if you are a Democrat or a Republican, a Socialist or a Capitalist, a Christian or a Moslem, an Idealist or a Pragmatist. What do matter are your attitudes and beliefs towards yourself. More precisely, your emotional and mental states affect your overall energy field; if your beliefs shape those emotional and mental states, then they are important. A common example of this is the belief or attitude of being unworthy, particularly of spiritual blessing or of the good things in life. Attitudes and beliefs that foster joy, self-acceptance and self-esteem have been shown to have a significant and important effect on a person's physical well-being, how rapidly they heal after surgery, how effectively their immune system works, and so on. By contrast, attitudes and beliefs that foster depression or low self-esteem have been shown

to have a deleterious effect. Some beliefs go further and turn a person against some aspect of himself or herself, creating an internal civil war that is definitely reflected in the state of their overall energy field.

This is a particular concern for Incarnational Spirituality and the incarnational worldview, for often people may have negative views about themselves because of being incarnated, having a physical body, or having a personality. All these things are felt to separate them from God or from spirit. The incarnational worldview is the opposite to this, finding in our embodied individualities a generative source of spiritual energy and value.

Whenever and however possible, having positive attitudes and helpful, empowering, and nourishing beliefs to draw upon is important as part of your subtle energy first aid kit. Life can be very challenging and difficult at times, but having a good self-image and good attitudes and confidence about your self can help keep your energy flowing, upbeat, and attuned.

3. **Positive Thinking.** We are often told about the importance of positive thinking and that our greater good depends on holding only positive thoughts and feelings. This can create a curious backlash of anger and fear towards ourselves when negative thoughts and feelings creep in, as they are bound to do if only by leakage from the collective. This double reaction of having a negative thought and then feeling negatively about ourselves because of that can definitely constrict our energy.

Positive thinking is not a club to hold over our heads. It might be better characterized as relaxed and open thinking, the kind of thinking and feeling that enables us to stay connected, expansive, and flowing. Paying attention to what's right in our life and in our world, for instance, can restore a sense of balance and positivity. However, while positive thinking can shift the surface characteristics of our energy field, what is really wanted is positive beingness, a general habit of thinking and feeling positively about oneself and the world. Having a negative thought, getting irritated or angry once in awhile, feeling down for a day or so, all these natural experiences that we can have will not sabotage or depress our energy field—though they can have a momentary effect on our surface energies; what is most important here is the consistency of our thinking and feeling over the long-term of months and years.

While holding positive thoughts and emotions is advantageous, positive thinking itself is not "Hallmark Card thinking." It's really an ongoing awareness that all truly is well with the world, with life, and with oneself. It's also a commitment not to mindlessly pass on fears but to bring positive energy, images, ideas, and feelings into the lives of others, to help them attune to the wellness at the heart of the world. If fear is the Balrog of our time, then positive thinking is like Gandalf standing courageously on the bridge deep in the mines of Moira saying, "You shall not pass!"

COMPARTMENT FOUR: ACTIONS

When we feel our energy is stuck or sluggish, often the best remedy is to take some action. There is an old maxim that says that energy follows thought, but as embodied beings, thought often follows action. I've already mentioned taking an energy walk or doing exercise. What I have in mind here is something more involved.

Sometimes our subtle energies can get bound up in our thinking. We have too many ideas, too many plans, too many thoughts in our head. Or we are bound up in our emotions. We feel the pressure of such accumulated energy. At such a time, what may help the most is just to take an action, that is, to do something.

This "something" shouldn't be "blind" or thoughtless, but it should focus thought in a particular way (and emotion, too, if they are feeling blocked). Imaging all the energy of your thinking and feeling bunched up like a group of people trying to get through a single narrow door. In this instance, it may not matter at all who goes through the door first, only that someone does so the traffic jam can be freed up and flow can be restored.

So, you might go gardening, or clean the kitchen, or build a model, or visit some part of your area you've always talked about seeing (residents of a place often don't ever see the landmarks in their vicinity that the tourists come to see); the action should be a simple task but demanding enough to require your attention and mindfulness, creating a focus of thought that energy can then flow along.

Even better is taking an action on behalf of someone else. An act of kindness, thoughtfulness, and helpfulness for another can have marvelously wonderful effects on your own energy field. Further, although the suggestions I'm offering are focused on you as a single person, the fact is that we all live in a larger ecology of life and consciousness. Our personal energy is part of the larger energy fields of our communities, of the land, indeed of the planet as a whole. When we act only out of self-concern and for our own personal ends exclusively, we disconnect ourselves from these larger energy fields with effects that over time are deleterious to our own subtle energy state. Recognizing that we are part of a larger whole and acting to benefit the world around us is a vital way to keep our own energy flowing, healthy, and connected.

The point here is that when energy feels blocked or stymied, taking an action can help unblock the flow.

COMPARTMENT FIVE: GROUNDING

Grounding essentially means connecting with a larger or more integrated system and sharing your energy with it. This is the first aid action of choice when we're experiencing more energy than we know what to do with, or with an intensity of energy—or sometimes even just with subtle energies that feel different and strange. If at any time I cannot integrate the energies I feel, that is when I should seek grounding.

The metaphor for grounding is a lightning rod which connects a house to the earth. If lightning strikes, all that energy which might set the house ablaze is channeled into the earth, which is large enough to absorb it without harm.

What constitutes a "larger system" can vary depending on the situation and the intensity and quality of the energy you may be experiencing; the techniques of grounding can vary, too. Here are some suggestions arranged according to the scale of the "ground" you are using, moving from "smallest" to "largest."

1. **Your body**. Sometimes all you need to do to "ground" or anchor an energy is to do something physical. I've already covered some of this when I talked about taking actions or lifestyle issues. Note that you're NOT deliberately trying to take energies into your body—unless you know what you're doing and how to transmute or deal with anything you take on, this can be dangerous. But sometimes your body will by its very nature absorb and participate in whatever energy field you are encountering.

One of the quickest, easiest, most effective ways of altering or grounding an excess of energy you may feel is to eat or drink something. Anything that stimulates your bodily processes and systems to do their own organic work—exercise can help here as well—will help disperse and ground those energies. One reason we can think of our bodies as systems for grounding is that they are highly integrated and already have organized systems for dealing with physical and subtle energies that have evolved over millions of years.

2. **Your mind and heart**. This harkens back to Compartments 1 and 3 dealing with identity and attitudes. Your mental and emotional state can provide a force for grounding unwanted or excess energies you may be feeling. One of the most effective ways of dispersing and grounding such energies is laughter. Watching a comedy or something that makes you laugh and generates good feeling is a powerful energy transforming and grounding process. Things you do that help you feel calm and peaceful or centered are also good, but be careful of meditative or metaphysical practices that might actually "tune you in" and invoke more energies at a time when you're dealing with an experience of too much energy or too different an energy. Your personality is in its own way a highly organized and integrated psychic system. Yes, people can be ungrounded in their personalities, in which case adding subtle energies to that mix can cause troubles. But a personality may be seen as a coherent pattern of connections with places, people and events, and within this coherency a stable and grounding center can be found.

3. **Your home environment**. Here the larger system into which you are "grounding" is familiarity and your connections with specific things that make up your usual environment. Home is usually where we live but wherever or whatever it is, it's a place where we can feel safe and upheld and hopefully where there's a sense of stability. It's a place that we feel is attuned to us. Often this is an actual house or apartment where we are surrounded by familiar and friendly things that have their own energy. All subtle energies have "vectors" in the sense of possessing momentum and direction or intent. Integration and grounding is sometimes simply a matter of changing the vector of an energy from one moving at cross-purposes to our lives or in a manner that is interfering or too intense to

one that is aligned and in harmony with the vectors of our own energy field. Home and familiar surroundings, whatever form they may take for us, represents a powerful momentum and vector aligned with us, one that can receive and redirect the flow and direction, quality and "spin" of energies that may be troubling us.

4. **The land and nature**. This is a big system indeed, and it is one that, I've found, people usually think of when they think of "grounding" energies. It's very common to find meditations and visualizations that contain some phrase like "let the energies flow through your legs into the ground" or "earth the energies through you into the earth below" or similar phrases and ideas. Nature is big, no question, larger than you or me, and it has a huge capacity to take on energy vectors and swallow them up. Putting one's hands in the soil is not only an action, as I discussed in Compartment Four, but also a way of letting excess energy flow from the body and into the ground.

5. **The Sacred**. The Sacred is the largest "ground" of all, and indeed is often referred to as the "ground of all being." Using the Sacred as a means of grounding an energy depends on your understanding of the Sacred and what your particular religious, spiritual, or philosophical stance allows. Still, this is the classic technique of "turning it over to God," where "it" can be not just a troubling problem but a troubling energy as well. The challenge is that if connection with the Sacred puts you into a high energy state, you may find yourself with more energy rather than less, again aggravating the situation. However, through faith, we expect that the intelligence of the Sacred knows what is needed, even if it's simply an inspiration to use one of the other methods I've discussed.

Whatever method or scale you use, the process of grounding is simple. You are directing a felt sense of energy, a flow of energy, a sensation of energy—however you are experiencing it—from within and around yourself into the larger, more stable, or more integrated system. You are release and directing the energy to flow from you into that which can more adequately and appropriately contain and alchemize it or redirect it away from you. This can be done as a simple act of imagination, visualizing and feeling the energy you don't want moving out from you and into whatever larger system (or systems, you could use more than one) you have selected to use.

COMPARTMENT SIX: INTENTIONALITY

Often the way to deal with any energy, whether arising from within yourself or coming from some place outside you, is with a strong intention and will on your part. This could be an intent to accept and embrace it or to turn it away or to transform it. Literally the very first lesson my own inner mentor, John, gave to me when we began working together, was that I could say NO to any being, force or energy I might feel if I didn't agree with it, want it, or feel ready for it. However, this "no" wasn't simply a word of refusal. It actually needed to be a strong energy of intent.

This is because what we call subtle energies may also be seen as flows and currents of information and intentionality that possess vectors, that is, direction, qualities, momentum, and the like. Our own intentions are also energy vectors backed up by the integrity and momentum of our own identity and will. Coherency, integration, and wholeness are all "vectors" in themselves which have a powerful momentum, a kind of "conservation of coherency." Wholeness has an inertia (a resistance to change) as well which can overcome an incoherent, detached, disconnected energy.

Standing in our Sovereignty (which is what the Standing exercise is about), aligning with and drawing upon the energy of our incarnational field, and expressing a clear intent sets forth a powerful internal energy that more often than not can redirect, transform, or transmute other energy bits that have attached to us.

What kind of intent am I talking about here? The intent need not be directed towards the offending or disturbing energy itself; I need not be confrontational here. The intent is more like a marshalling and directing of my energies towards some task or goal or inner state different from that of the energy that is affecting me. This sets into motion a momentum and flow that either brings the offending or disturbing energy into align with me (thereby being transformed) or moves it out of my field. The point is that I give my attention and thought to my intent and take it off the offending energy, and where my attention goes, my own energy soon follows.

A FINAL NOTE

As I said at the beginning, these "compartments" in this first aid kit and the suggestions within them are just that, only suggestions. If they spark insights for you, that's wonderful; if they inspire you with things you can do to deal with any difficult energies within yourself in the moment, that is their purpose. They are not meant in any way to be an exhaustive list of possibilities but rather illustrations of principles.

In creating "subtle energy first aid" responses of our own, remember that healthy energies are flowing, circulating, connected, coherent, benevolent, and generative. These are guidelines to the qualities and affects you want the energies you experience and embody to have. Hopefully they will give you insights in how to handle the energy phenomena that may arise within you.

SUBTLE ACTIVISM

[In 2009, I wrote the following booklet as a short, small document that Lorian could send out to individuals who were writing in asking about ways of working with subtle energies to bless the world. The material is still relevant and up-to-date ten years later.]

An Energy Ecology

We live in a world filled with energies of all kinds. Some are the electromagnetic forces that light our lights and heat our stoves and bring us voices over the radio and images on our televisions. But there are other energies that surround us as well, of which most of us are probably unaware but which can affect us just as powerfully. These are *subtle* forces generated by life, consciousness and spirit.

Where do these energies come from?

They can come from natural sources, from the land, from the sea, from the sun and stars. They come from spiritual sources and ultimately from the Sacred. They come from living beings, from microbes and bacteria, from plants like trees and grass, from animals, and from people—from the whole biomass of the earth.

Many of these subtle energies come from the activity of consciousness, the radiation of thoughts and feelings from human beings.

These are meta-physical energies, and they are as much a part of our surroundings as the physical ones with which we are more familiar. They flow between people and between us and our environment. They form an energy ecology that can affect our feelings, our thoughts, and our overall well-being and vitality in both positive and negative ways.

It's an ecology that we participate in creating through our thoughts, our emotions, and our physical activity, often now in major ways as humanity's influence and technological prowess upon the earth has increased. We bear a responsibility for the health and wellbeing of this subtle ecology and for its impact upon the world. The exercise of this responsibility is **subtle activism.**

Energy Connections

In the physical world, we are separated by distance. What happens to someone on the far side of the earth may seem to have little consequence or affect upon me. We believe our thoughts and feelings are private, locked within our skulls and our skins. But in the energy world, we are all connected in profound and interdependent ways. It's as if we were all standing on a great trampoline. When one person bounces, it makes the whole trampoline move and we all bounce to some degree. Subtle energies are not limited by distance. Thus when a calamity strikes in some part of the world, our energy bodies all feel the effect of the suffering and fear no matter where we are. We may feel uneasy or restless, anxious or fearful for no reason we can see.

We live in turbulent, troubling times. The news is filled with one crisis after another from war and terrorism to economic turmoil to global climate change. Through our technological ability to communicate images, thoughts, and feelings quickly and dramatically, we can share our thoughts and feelings—particularly our fears, anxieties, angers, hatreds, and pessimism—around the world with greater intensity, increasing the impact of the subtle energies these thoughts and feelings generate. Such energies are repeated, reinforced, and strengthened by both global media and our subtle energy connections until they accumulate in our world. If they are positive images and energies, they can be an inspiration and upliftment for us all, but if, as they usually are, they are negative in tone and quality, they become a psychic pollution weighing upon all of us. Such subtle pollution, like its physical counterpart, can obstruct the flow and expression of healthy energies and can be a source of further distress. It can poison the mental and emotional environment in which it is found and feed the energies of conflict in the world.

In addition, there are conditions and places in the world where great evil has been done, where suffering has been perpetuated, where hatred, fear, anger, and violence have been cultivated for generations between people. There the land itself is soaked in subtle energies of conflict and pain, continuing to influence human affairs until healing and forgiveness can take place.

Subtle Activism

Subtle activism is a procedure for dealing with this psychic pollution and poison. It is a way of working with your own subtle energies and spiritual resources to create a clear, clean, positive, vibrant and healthy energy environment in places of trouble and difficulty in the world.

43

When this procedure is used to deal with psychic pollution within and around yourself, then it becomes energy hygiene. Energy hygiene is simply subtle activism at a personal level.

Not a Substitute

Subtle activism is not a substitute for taking action and doing good in wise and compassionate ways in the physical world. Physical activism is necessary for we live in a world where pain and suffering, hunger and disease, oppression and injustice, pollution and environmental degradation have real physical manifestations and consequences. Subtle energy activism is not *instead of* but *in addition to* work and effort to heal the world and ourselves.

However, because it's invisible to most people, the earth's second ecology of the subtle energy world can go underestimated and ignored. Yet its effects when negative can hinder and diminish outer efforts at helping in the world and even create or intensify imbalance and negativity in the world. Conversely, when positive its effects can support and enhance the good efforts of physical activists to relieve suffering and injustice.

Subtle energy activism is not a substitute, but it is an important complement to outer activism. More importantly, in many cases when the cause of suffering and imbalance originates or is perpetuated in the energy realm, it may be the only form of activism that can effectively make a difference.

More than Cleansing or Fixing

Subtle activism is much more than just process of rescuing, fixing, or cleansing. It's about creating, vitalizing and expressing wholeness. It's about honoring and nourishing sovereignty, identity, coherency, and boundaries on the one hand and developing and practicing connectedness, engagement, love, and a compassionate participation in life on the other. In its full expression, it's a practice of "walking whole" and living your potential as a generative source of blessing in the world. Energy activism is the expression of an incarnational spirituality.

THREE BASIC RULES
OF GOOD SUBTLE ENERGY ACTIVISM.

1. DON'T IMPOSE: We each have our own personal energies, our own opinions and ideas about how the world should be and how people should live for their highest good. We resent it when someone else tries to impose their way of being, thinking, and doing upon us, particularly if it's very different from our own. When we are in trouble, we may need help, but we resist being thought of as something to be "fixed." We want and need help in a form that honors and respects our own sovereignty, that empowers us to develop our own capacities, that helps us to grow, and enables us as much as possible to find our own solutions to the problems. We want assistance but we want empowerment as well.

This is true in any situation. The subtle energy activist doesn't seek to impose his or her "way" or energies upon a situation but to create openness for the innate spirit, health, and wisdom within people to emerge and express in a manner unique to them and appropriate to the situation.

2. STAY CONNECTED: Dealing with the psychic pollution and negative subtle energies of the world is not something any person can do on his or her own, any more than one person could clear away all the rubble and rescue all the survivors in a town devastated by an earthquake. We need allies. We need to be connected to the larger spirit of wholeness in the earth. We need to be aligned and connected with the Sacred. If we don't have any physical allies to work with, we can seek out allies of a spiritual nature who themselves live and work within the realms of subtle energy. And we need to work with the souls and energies of those whom we seek to help.

3. BE INCLUSIVE: Sometimes, a person drawn to energy activism sees himself or herself as a "warrior of Light" going forth to do battle with "forces of darkness." It's easy to frame a situation so that there are "friends" to help and "enemies" to combat. But subtle energy activism is not spiritual combat. It is an act of healing, which is inclusive by its nature. There are no enemies in energy activism, only conditions to be understood, held in love and positive energies, and transformed.

There are many techniques of energy activism, many different ways in which individuals and groups can participate in this endeavor. But at its core, energy activism is a process of creating wholeness. Not imposing, forming connections, staying connected, and being inclusive are all simply ways of doing so.

An Exercise

Energy activism can take many forms depending on the situation, the people involved, the intent, and so forth. Here is a very simple and generic exercise. It is not directed towards any particular situation but towards holding, "grounding" and integrating a sphere of blessing that can spread throughout the energy world contributing to healing the negative elements therein.

Imagine the pain, the suffering, the hostility and violence, the anger and hatred, all the negative thoughts and feelings of humanity as a dark and turbulent layer surrounding the world. Don't attune to this or try to enter it in any way but just picture it as a layer of dark storm clouds overhead covering the earth.

Now imagine a sphere of light like a globe surrounding the world. It's as if a golden sphere of radiance from the sun has crossed space and is now enfolding the earth, including the dark, stormy layer of negativity.

Picture this sphere of golden, healing, invigorating light seeking to blend and dissolve into the earth to bring blessings to all life, but it bounces off the layer of darkness. The storm clouds prevent it from coming through.

Ground yourself by finding your own unique peace and strength. In whatever way feels comfortable and right to you, attune to the inner light within yourself. Feel this light unfold and expand until it surrounds you as your own sphere of golden light.

Extend a thread of this light downward into the earth, into the spiritual light at the heart of the world, the spirit of the earth, of Gaia. Link with this inner, peaceful, life-giving light of the earth letting it enhance and increase the radiance of the sphere of light around you.

Now extend a thread of light from the sphere around you upward through the stormy clouds to the golden sphere of light beyond them. Let your light connect to it. You and your light are now a connection between the heart of the world and this sphere of golden radiance and blessing.

Around the world are thousands of people doing just what you're doing, finding ways to bring light to earth to harmonize with the world, heal the darkness and bring blessings to all in loving and compassionate ways. Picture these people on every continent, each encased in his or her own sphere of light, each drawing upon the light within the earth, each connected to the golden sphere around the earth. Imagine a clear light of connection going from your heart to each of them, forming a vast net of human jewels, each sparkling with inner light, each connected to the heart of the world, each connected to the sphere of light above us.

At this point there's nothing you need to do. You simply need to hold the connection between yourself, the earth, the sphere of light, and others around the world sharing your concerns and attunements. You are like the stake anchoring a tent to the ground. Your job is to remain anchored, balanced, part of the earth, part of humanity, connected to the world around you, the people around you, and the life within yourself. Your job is to remain integrated and whole. The golden light of blessing surrounding the world knows what to do. It has the task of acting. You have the task of holding.

As you gracefully and peacefully hold your connections, releases this mediation and go about your daily activities in ordinary ways. As you hold your connectedness in your heart and remain integrated with the world through your daily life, this golden sphere of light can descend, past the storm clouds, breaking up and healing the seeds of negativity feeding the storm clouds. This light, connected to the earth through your life and the lives of those like you sharing this task of holding, can now draw itself to earth, bringing blessing in its wake, moving through and dispersing the clouds and becoming a healing part of the planet we all share. It knows what to do, and it will do it.

EXCEPTS FROM
VIEWS FROM THE BORDERLAND
ISSUE 30 (DECEMBER, 2018)

[Four times a year, I publish a journal, Views from the Borderland, in which I share my "field notes" from my contacts and explorations with the subtle worlds and with the subtle beings who live within them. These journals cover a wide variety of topics, but Issue 30, December 2018, focused exclusively on the nature of the challenges facing humanity at a subtle energetic level and how we might cope with them. Here are some excerpts from that issue.]

Our Inner Star

For me, all subtle work begins with attunement to our generative nature. This is one of the key insights of Incarnational Spirituality. Each of us is a generative source of Light. It's as if we are a power plant or, in my favorite metaphor, a star. A star generates light and heat because of the nuclear fusion going on within it; there is a process at work that makes a star radiant.

There is a process going on within us as well, an incarnational process, which makes us radiant, too. Just as a star has its own spectrographic signature, so each of us generates and radiates Light in a unique way. I call this our "Self-Light." I call it this not simply because it is part of who we are but because it is an expression of the processes that *make* us who we are. It is the Light that emerges from the incarnational act of "self-making" or "Selfing."

This Self-Light is not simply a by-product, though. It is an objective, a purpose, a design feature of the incarnational act which, whatever else it may produce, is intended to create a generative source of Light and spiritual presence within the incarnate realm.

We are that source.

We are used to thinking of Light as something we invoke, something we draw down upon ourselves from higher realms of Spirit. There *is* Light or spiritual energy and presence that can be drawn into our lives, into our world, from a variety of spiritual sources. But Self-Light comes from us, from the act of being here in the world. We don't have to access any other source to have it.

The reality of Self-Light means that we have to think of ourselves in new ways. We are not just consumers; we are producers. We are not simply deliverers of the gifts of spiritual Light from other sources, like traders and merchants importing wonders from distant shores; we are craftspersons who offer wares of our own making, our own creation. We are generative sources of Light: of spiritual blessing and vital energies of life.

Acknowledging this is an important step into accepting and developing the innate spiritual power of who we are. Another such step is acknowledging our Sovereignty.

In Incarnational Spirituality, Sovereignty is my word for the will-to-be and the resultant clarity and strength of our spiritual Identity. It is our ability to be self-governing and to hold the processes of self-making that generate our Self-Light. In a way, Sovereignty is like the mass of the star that triggers and maintains the nuclear fusion that in turn produces energy in the form of light and heat. It is the sanctity of being who we are in a way that enables our incarnational identity to unfold its generative nature. It is an expression of the will of the Soul that makes incarnational possible and defines its nature.

There are a variety of exercises in Incarnational Spirituality—which you can explore through books I've written, like *Journey into Fire*, or through classes that Lorian offers—for attuning to and standing in Sovereignty and Self-Light. They boil down to acknowledging as a felt sense within you, within your body, and not just as an abstraction or intellectual idea, the value and importance of being who you are, the rightness of loving who you are, and the recognition that you have something to give the world that no one else can give. They enable you to see your subtle nature as a radiant source and yourself as a "star" of Light, a producer, not just a consumer. There are many ways you can come to this realization and acknowledgement; Incarnational Spirituality is just one way. For convenience sake, though, I include the basic Self-Light exercise at the end of this issue.

As a subscriber to this Journal, you may already be familiar with Sovereignty and Self-Light. I bring it up because the other tools I suggest we have to be a help in the world and to maintain our own integrity and balance all draw on the nature of our Self as embodied in these two concepts. Whatever is happening in the world, both positively and negatively, it cannot take our Sovereignty and Self-Light from us or diminish them unless we condescend to that loss and diminishment.

We are an inner star, and from this star-ness comes our ability to server and help in the subtle dimensions and in the physical world as well.

Physical Action

It is important to affirm that subtle action is a complement to and not a substitute for physical action. We are physical beings with thoughts and feelings, and we live in a world that is responsive to these things. We are incarnated precisely to take advantage of our physical and psychological abilities in service to the world.

Sometimes we are in a position where our physical action can directly help. First responders fall into this category. A fireman is in a position to put out a wildfire, for instance, or a police officer to stop a shooter or halt a crime. A person with a boat may rescue people whose homes are flooded after a storm.

Likewise, sometimes we are in a position where we can directly affect the subtle atmosphere and energy field where help is needed. For example, a nurse may do this everyday by bringing a spirit of hope, comfort, and healing into the hospital where she works. A teacher may do this by creating an open and encouraging atmosphere in his classroom, one in which children feel honored and listened to and excited about learning.

On the other hand, there are always events happening in the world that are too distant from where we are or they require skills and physical attributes we may not have. We have no easy or accessible way of taking physical action. This is when we may feel helpless, especially if they are events in which people are suffering. Likewise, we can see or imagine the psychological trauma inflicted by such events, by loss, death, pain, and fear. Yet we're not on the scene to give comfort. This, too, can make us feel powerless.

What is important to realize is that we are not powerless. We can always take physical action to bring blessing into the world. We can always take subtle actions to bring Light into the world. Doing one may well empower and enhance doing the other. We are never helpless on either front. Such actions, even if seemingly unrelated to the far distant events that triggered our concern, can still become a catalyst for healing even at a distance.

There are two aspects to this. The first is determining what we can do on a physical level to bring positive energies into our world. The trip to the grocery store that I wrote about in the last issue of *Views* is one example of this drawn from my own life. Perhaps one of the most powerful actions we can take is a simple act of kindness. Some years ago, a good friend of mine, Andy Smallman, invited me to join him in creating an online kindness class. He and my oldest son, John-Michael, had been teaching a kindness class at the school Andy founded, where Johnny was a student. This class had been so successful, Andy wanted to make it available over the Internet. At the time, though, my plate was full and I felt unable to take him up on his invitation. My loss! Andy went on to become a major force in the kindness movement in this country. You can follow his work, and his free online kindness classes, at www. kindliving.net. (In a similar vein, I also recommend the book *Angels on Earth* by Laura Schroff for truly inspiring examples of the transformative power of simple acts of kindness.)

Acts of kindness, generosity, blessing—even of ordinary civility and courtesy—have an energetic ripple effect. Anytime we can bring a smile into another's life, something good is let loose in the world. It may not seem like much, but cumulatively, it can be very powerful. We add to a reservoir of positive subtle energy that spiritual allies can draw upon to use in places we might not expect. And, as Laura Schroff shows in her book, such acts can have far reaching physical life effects beyond our immediate knowledge.

Kindness power can never be underestimated. Truly, it is a superpower.

The second aspect of taking physical action relates to the power of resonance. There is a simple equation here. Subtle energy is amplified when generated by our whole being through felt sense and not just through our mind or will alone. In turn, this felt sense is anchored and expanded through appropriate and resonate physical action.

Let me give you an example of what I mean. Let's say I read about threats to the Brazilian rainforest. There's little I can do physically to deter these threats, though I might seek out an organization that is able to do so and see how I can support them. However, I want to do subtle activism, generating and sending Light to enhance the protection of the forest. So, I form an image in my mind of the rainforest and visualize it surrounded by Light. The problem is that my mind is very useful for focusing energy—it makes an excellent lens—but it's not that powerful as a generator. After all, it's only part of my whole generative self from which my Self-Light radiates. It's as if I wanted to focus a beam of light to illuminate a darkened space, but while the lens was working well, the bulb that produced the light was dim due to a lack of sufficient electrical energy.

There is another problem. My tendency will be to think of myself as doing something to protect the rainforest, in this case, sending Light and positive subtle energies. But in fact, for this protection to be powerful and effective, it is the spirit of the rainforest that needs to do it. Put another way, a protective energy arising from the plants and trees of the rainforest itself is more grounded in the affected environment and potentially more powerful than any protective energy I can generate and send from a distance. The better way to think about this act of subtle activism is that I am acting as a catalyst that triggers or empowers the spiritual forces of the rainforest to be active and protective.

What I am leading to here is that my act of subtle activism begins with me standing in my Sovereignty and Self-Light—my awareness of myself as a generative source—and then engaging with a plant or tree in my immediate physical surroundings. I go to a tree or I sit with a house plant and I extend my blessing and Self-Light to it. I hold that plant in love and I ask the spirit of that plant or tree to join with me in creating an aura or field of safety around it, one to which it contributes. I pay attention to what happens in me, in my energy field, as this occurs. What is the felt sense of protection, safety, love, caring, and life that is stirred in me by enacting a protective and loving relationship to this plant.

You might say I am asking this particular plant or tree to translate my human intent to protect the rainforest into "plant-speak," into an energy resonant with this plant or trees ability to protect itself and affirm its life, and I pay attention to how this feels in my body and in my whole being.

It is this felt sense that I then use to generate a connection to the spirit of the rainforest. It's like offering a homeopathic "pill" of protection that then triggers a larger, systemic response within the subtle field of the rainforest itself. I go in a subtle way to the rainforest cloaked in the energy of a relationship I have just built with a specific plant in my own environment, an energy that embodies in miniature what I would like the field of the rainforest to embody as a much larger system.

The principle here is a simple one. Physical action is often an important component of subtle action (and vice versa), the two strengthening and energizing each other. In this example, I act physically with something in my environment to invoke the kind of subtle energy I want to offer somewhere else in the world through subtle activism; I pay attention to and hold within myself the felt sense that arises from that action, and then I use that felt sense for give power to my inner action. The physical act helps to define and boost the subtle action.

The reverse is also true. I can stand in my Self-Light and find within myself a place of peace or of love, of caring or of compassion, and then use that energy to inform my physical actions, no matter how simple they may seem. A nurse who is attuned to her Presence and Self-Light automatically brings that energy as a blessing to her patients, for example. We are whole, interconnected systems, and one part of us can be used to enhance other parts, increasing our generativity in the process.

Our Personal Subtle Energy Field

Our personal subtle energy field is our means for working with subtle forces and engaging with subtle allies. It holds and expresses our Self-Light, our spiritual presence and power, within the subtle environment around us and the subtle dimensions of the world. It is like our physical skin and our immune system combined, providing defense against subtle energies in the environment that might be disruptive to our energetic coherency and integrity.

Our subtle energy fields can be buffeted and "shivered" by negative energies in the world that people and events generate, what I think of as the "damndruff" of our physical, mental and emotional lives. They are normally robust and able to throw off or transmute what might otherwise attach itself to us, like dirt to our skins. But sustained stressful energies of fear, anger, hatred, and the like, such as many people are exposed to on a daily basis through the news media, can begin to wear down our natural defenses. Likewise, when our own thinking and feeling is disturbed and upset, the subtle field reflects that and becomes more vulnerable. We can weaken our own internal subtle immune system, just as we can our physical one.

We clean our bodies of the day's accumulation of dirt and we do things to strengthen ourselves and our immune systems physically. We can do the same with our subtle body and its field. Doing so is an act of power, one that demonstrates we are not helpless in the world. We can make our subtle field a clear transmitter of our Self-Light and the energies of blessing. It just requires our intention and our attention.

I do not have the space in this journal, given the other topics I wish to cover, to go into a full description of energy hygiene, the activities that can keep our subtle field clear and clean; for that, I direct you to my book, *Working with Subtle Energies.* But there are some simple, basic techniques that I can pass on to you here.

The key principle here is that our subtle energy field reflects and to some extent is shaped by what we are thinking and especially by what we are feeling. It's not the momentary thought or feeling that is important here but our overall habits of thought and emotion, the kind of psychological state that is our norm. Think of it this way. If I walk across a grassy meadow once or twice, the grass will be bent when my feet have stepped on it, showing my path, but fairly quickly, it will straighten back to the way it was. At that point, there is no indication that I have walked across the meadow. That sudden burst of irritation or fear or that momentary surge of affection or gratitude will ripple through our subtle field and then vanish, its effect on our field gone.

But if I consistently walk through the meadow and I take the same route each time, the grass will be broken down and a path will be trodden into the earth, one that remains to show where I have walked and the direction I have taken. Likewise, if I am consistent in my loving intention and attention or in my fearful or angry moods, then these qualities and patterns become habits of flow within the subtle field. Those that are "negative" can create constraining and conflicting patterns that obstruct the clear expression of our Self-Light, whereas a habit of positive emotions and thought in relationship to the world and to oneself heightens the ability of our subtle field to transmit our spiritual energies and presence.

For this reason, one simple, practical, and powerful exercise we can do—one that I do daily—is to take a moment to love ourselves. I don't mean this in a narcissistic way, nor do I mean just a simple feeling of affection or approval for oneself. Love is at the heart of our incarnation;

it is the soul quality, more than any other, that ultimately inspires us to take incarnation. There may be other reasons, good and important reasons, for being born into this world, but the motivating force behind them that powers the soul's "will-to-incarnate" is love.

My moment of loving myself—my occasional "Love Break" in the midst of the day's activities—is a moment of tuning in to this soul force within me. It is remembering that love is the force behind my incarnation, that it empowers me and strengthens me. My life matters and has value because, in whatever way I can, I can bring this love into the world.

Attuning to this force of love within me, I visualize it filling and blessing my physical body, my psyche, and my subtle body and energy field. I hold all of me in this love, remembering that *this* is who I am, this is who we all are. This is the power we all hold within us.

I can feel anger, hurt, fear, and distress as much as anyone; I don't try to be immune to normal human emotions. But I don't identify with any of them. What I identify with is the love at the heart of my incarnation, at the heart of all our incarnations. My "Love Breaks" help me reinforce this; they are the path I trod through the meadow so that love becomes a habit, not an occasional deliverance. It's purely a matter of practice. That we can do this practice and that it has an effect within us is part of our power, part of why we are not helpless before the world.

There is no question our subtle field can be buffeted by negative energies in the environment and the world around us. In the past, this most likely was not so large an issue, but now, through social media, the Internet, cyberspace, cellphones, television, and radio, we are immersed in a continuous field of information and stimulation, much of which is simply noise and static. We are more exposed to people's negative projections—their "damndruff"—as, for example, through social media, than ever before. Screens are everywhere, in everyone's pocket or in their hands, telling us this, telling us that, warning us, attacking us, cajoling us, propagandizing us, informing us.

Never before in human history has so much information been thrust so quickly and continuously upon so many. We are deluged with information, much of which beseeches us to be something other than who we are, to think or feel in a certain way, or to buy what we don't really need. Much of it—maybe most of it—comes with very little meaning and depth to it. It is simply emotional and mental stimulation, frequently driven by dramatic narratives that demand our attention, our allegiance, our outrage, or our sorrow.

This is only the surface. The subtle environment of the earth is just as alive with waves of information stimulated by human activity and by profound changes taking place in the subtle patterns and currents of the planet. It isn't just the physical climate that is changing; the inner "climate" is changing, too.

What is becoming increasingly scarce in our technological society is silence, moments and places where all the information, all the projections, all the noise stops. Interestingly, in some circumstances and places, silence is becoming a luxury commodity to sell, as, for instance, in airports where high-priced lounges guarantee a place to go where there is quiet: no electronic devices, no Internet, no noise, just silence.

We can feel helpless before this onslaught of information and noise, but this is an illusion. We always have the power to power down our devices, shut down the cellphone, turn off the television and radio. We can create pockets of silence for ourselves. We owe it to the health and calm functioning of our subtle energy field to do so, to give ourselves not just Love Breaks but Silence Breaks as well.

I'm fortunate in this regard in that I work at home and can thus create a quiet environment as and when I wish. But the majority of people in our society do not have this option. There must be an intentional practice to take a moment of silence now and again.

The kind of information that comes to us these days through media, whether television, the Internet, our smartphones, or whatever, is choppy, usually in small bits. Our attention spans grow shorter and shorter, and information is delivered in smaller and smaller units. Stories in the news flash by: one week it's the flooding in Texas, then in Florida, then in Puerto Rico; now it's about the President's twitter war with members of his own party. But wait, what about Texas again? It's out of the news completely.

Life is not like that, though. We don't live in short paragraphs but in long narratives. To the people in Houston, Harvey and the flooding continue to have effects and will for some time; even more so for those in Puerto Rico and the Virgin Islands. Yet through our media, our attention is dragged away and onto something else, the story of the day, of the hour, of the minute.

The energies of Spirit are what I think of as "long waves." Our soul is a "long wave," too. To attune to these levels of being, we need to find that inner quiet that can allow us to listen to those long waves. We need to allow our attentiveness and awareness to spread out again, to grow large. We need to find in Silence a home for infinity and eternity, a place beyond time, beyond the chatter of the moment.

This is really what the Silence means to me: not just quiet per se but an inner space of attunement to the long rhythms of life, to a spaciousness that allows our spirit—and Spirit in general—to have elbow room. It means stepping out of the cramped little boxes of information and narrative, images, feelings, and thoughts that make up the offerings of modern media.

To paraphrase the Womenfolk, one of my favorite folk-singing groups from the Sixties, we are spacious beings living in a culture of "ticky, tacky, little boxes." Taking time for Silence, for stillness, for quiet, allows us to remember and reconnect with that spaciousness. We can begin to decompress.

Just as importantly, it allows us time and space to digest. We can get so much information, it's hard to process it all. It's like eating and eating and eating, without taking time to assimilate what we've taken in and make it part of us. Doing this makes us ill.

As implied above, taking a "Silence Break" doesn't necessarily mean finding a quiet spot, however helpful that may be. It means shifting out of the time-bound, moment-by-moment, short attention span of the personality into a timeless, spacious place. It means recognizing our larger Self that embraces the world but is not defined or limited by the chatter that fills it. In this, it is not too different from the Love Break I described. The two can certainly be combined.

Nor need it be long, at least as far as the subtle field is concerned. As much as I might like an hour or two of peace and quiet, a minute or so of attunement to Love, Silence, and the Spacious Spirit can have an immediate effect on our subtle field. It exists and operates in a dimension that is less bound to time and space as we know them, and for most of us, it is very resilient, able to change quickly.

There is a third practice that I find not only helpful in restoring calm and power to my subtle field but in reminding me that I am never helpless, never powerless. Many of you are familiar with this practice through classes and books in Incarnational Spirituality. I call it the Touch of Love.

Basically, this is a practice of taking the spirit and force of love I attune to at the core of my being and passing it on into my environment through something that I touch. If I'm sitting at a desk, I touch the desk; if I'm relaxing with a cup of coffee, I touch the coffee cup; if I'm sitting in a chair, I touch the chair. Wherever I am, whatever I'm doing, there's something I can touch, even if it's just the floor under my feet. Whatever I touch, I allow the love to which I have attuned to flow through me and into it.

There are two reasons why this is important. The first is that healthy subtle energies are in motion; they are flowing. Love is not something I can bottle up inside and keep to myself; its very nature demands that it be shared, that it flow out to join the world. To attune to love means, to me, also allowing it to flow out. As Shakespeare's Juliet says, "My bounty is as boundless as the sea, my love as deep. The more I give to thee, the more I have, for both are infinite." If I tune into the sea of love, I cannot hope to keep it confined. It must flow out.

The second reason is that the love I share with whatever object I'm touching and its subtle field ripples outward into the subtle environment, triggering and heightening love and blessing as it does so. Something happens. Change takes place. It may be a minor change, it may be a major change, but the subtle environment, and perhaps the physical one as well, is not the same as it was.

Our psyches straddle the physical and subtle worlds. Anchored in our physical brains, our thoughts and emotions reach into and are part of the subtle dimension. Our psychological states and activities are always linked to the subtle environment, just as they are to the physical environment. Conditions existing in the subtle environment can affect the thinking and feeling of those within its influence and vice versa. Again, the effect may be minor, it may be cumulative, or it may be significant in the moment.

The point is that by altering the energetic conditions of the subtle environment, we can affect the psychological states of people, including ourselves, who are in that environment. Sending blessing and love into the subtle environment, however we may do so, is no small thing. It is an act of power that can make a difference, as many people have experienced. Again, we are never entirely helpless. We are always a generative presence in the subtle world around us and in its relationship to the physical world it pervades.

To summarize, all three of these practices—Love Break, Silence Break, and Touch of Love—affirm who we are as sacred individuals; they are acts of remembrance as well as moments of attunement and subtle action. Taken as a whole, the felt sense of these practices empowers us to stand in our wholeness and identity as generative sources of spiritual energies. They affirm that we are stars radiating the blessings of our Self-Light.

The Local Subtle Environment

This brings us to the local subtle environment, that part of the subtle worlds that is most closely tied to and reflects the physical environment around us. The subtle life around us can be a wonderful ally, helping to hold and augment our own subtle energy field through the connections we form.

I've already written much about the subtle environment in my books *Subtle Worlds* and *Working with Subtle Energies*. I don't want to repeat myself here. What I wish to share is an experience I had recently that gave me new insights into the nature of the subtle environment and the role it can play both in helping us deal with stressful energies in our world and in empowering our ability to counter such energies with our Self-Light.

I had turned off the television after watching a news report and was sitting in my living room, thinking about the distressful and fearful things that were happening in the world. I don't remember now just what particular incident I was focused on. In a way, it doesn't matter. These days, almost every news report tells of something awful happening somewhere in the world! What matters is that as I was sitting there thinking and feeling bad about what I'd seen, a being appeared. It seemed to step through the wall from outside my house and into the living room.

This being had the head and torso of a young, human male, but from the waist down, it was just a swirl of color and energy, as if it were emerging out of a mist. This was not in itself unusual; when I see subtle beings, I usually only see a head and features. Why waste energy shaping a whole body when it's not necessary in order to communicate?

I knew immediately that this being was not one of my normal subtle colleagues. It introduced itself a spokesperson for the subtle environment of the neighborhood where I live. This local subtle environment is filled with nature spirits associated with specific plants and trees or with elements of the landscape, such as a nearby lake or the foothills that surround us. But it also has beings who seem to serve the subtle environment of the neighborhood itself. They are like etheric ombudsmen, seeking to keep the flow of vital energies balanced, circulating, and helpful to both the human and non-human lives. This being was one of those.

Without preamble, this being said, "You are feeling unsafe. Do you feel a threat from the neighborhood?"

Taken aback, I said, "No. Nothing here is threatening me."

"Then let its energy uphold and strengthen you," it said.

At this point, the being reached out and touched me. I felt a force pushing me backwards, out of my body, and I found my awareness expanding out into the subtle environment around my house.

Immediately, I felt immersed in a strength and calm that seemed rooted in the earth. Where I had been feeling distressed, now I felt at peace. I felt solidly, deeply anchored in the moment and in this place, held by an active community of life.

This experience did not last long. Still embraced in this calm connectedness, I became aware again of being in my living room with this neighborhood spirit in front of me. It nodded and said, "Be where your body is, not only where your mind goes." Then, apparently satisfied, it disappeared.

Ever since my first subtle ally and mentor, John, had advised me back in the Sixties to make my environment my ally, I've had a practice of tuning in to my surrounding with love and gratefulness and anchoring myself in its presence. It's something I teach as part of learning to work with subtle energies. But I'd never felt anything quite as powerful and supportive as what I felt in this experience. It had a depth that was different from what I had previously experienced, as if an extra dimension had been added.

I gained insight into what this difference was a few days later, but before I share this, I want to say more about the immediate effect of this experience.

Over the past few years, I've gone through a number of surgeries and other procedures dealing with bladder cancer and resulting kidney damage. This often meant going through periods of intense pain. Pain has a way of focusing your attention, and it was easy to slip into thinking about myself and my body in terms of the parts that were damaged and suffering. But one day, one of my subtle colleagues reminded me that most of my body was healthy and working just fine. If I focused on the healthy parts, I could draw healing energies and help for the unhealthy parts, plus I would see myself as a healthy person with painful bits rather than simply as a sick person consumed by pain.

This shift in perspective was hugely helpful for me. Not only did it diminish the pain and, I believe, speed up the healing, but it put me back into an expanded and more spacious experience of myself, always a good thing! I still had the pain, but it wasn't defining me.

It seemed to me this is what this neighborhood spirit was telling me as well. What he did was to redirect my attention away from horrible happenings in a distant place, which were creating stress in my mind, to peaceful and supporting happenings in the place where my body was. "Be where my body is, not where my mind goes." By so doing, I was able to tap into a resource of subtle energies, being generated by the life in the environment around me, that was vitalizing and strengthening. I traded feeling helpless in the face of events elsewhere in the world beyond my physical ability to help to feeling empowered by a world I *could* tune into and affect.

I want to be clear here that this being was not saying, "Don't think about things that aren't here where you are. Don't worry or be concerned about things out there in the world." Instead, I took from what he showed me that I should not lose touch with my wholeness, part of which is in touch, through my mind and imagination, with distant events, and part of which is in touch with the energies of the land and of nature and of the Techno-elementals right here where my body is. I need to use the latter to give myself balance and strength to confront the former.

We tend to think in binary either/or ways: the world and humanity are either going to hell in a handbasket or a new world is being born in our midst and humanity will meet successfully the challenges we are facing. We can be pessimists or we can be optimists. But both these things are true. Death and birth, suffering and joy, chaos and harmony, imbalance and balance are all happening at the same time. If part of the planetary body is in pain, we can't deny it or turn away from it, but we can't define ourselves or Gaia by it alone, without risking disempowerment and a sense of helplessness. We can attune to the parts that are healthy, joyous, harmonious, and balanced, and from their strength, gain the power to hold and heal the parts that are suffering.

My neighborhood spirit was saying that, from its point of view, the subtle environment where it and I lived was healthy. Therefore, I could draw healthy energies and a sense of safety from it that would enable me to deal with events in the human world that were not healthy and that generated images and energies of non-safety and threat.

Subtle Perspectives

It has been interesting to me that over the past three months, when, with storms, floods, fires, violence, contentious elections, and wars, there has been so much turmoil in the world, my subtle colleagues have been consistent in keeping me focused on the subtle environment around me. Although events would seem to call out for it, I've done very little subtle activism during this period. When I try, I am gently but firmly redirected back to where I am. Finally, I asked my subtle colleagues about this. Three of them responded. For convenience, I shall call them Phillip, Marcus, and Mary. They come from three different frequencies of life and consciousness, and each brings a different perspective.

> **PHILLIP**: If you were building a campfire, you would not start with a large pile of logs. You would begin with that which is most accessible to the fire and most likely to burn easily. Once the flame was there, you would add your kindling, also easy to burn but able to hold the flame. That becomes the foundation for larger pieces of wood which can burn longer and hold the fire more hotly. Only at that point, when you have a fire able to sustain itself and not become extinguished by trying to burn too large a load, do you add the logs.
>
> Begin with what you can easily bless and engage with your Light and build up from there. Your environment knows you and will respond readily, for you are already in resonance with it simply by being in it. It is kindling waiting for your love. If your Light burns steady where you are, those who deal with planetary needs will know where to find your fire when they need it to nourish their greater flames.

MARCUS: I would point out two reasons for directing your attention locally. Both have to do with how you deal with the energies of life and spirit moving through your world. On the one hand, you are confronting negative energies arising from the shadows of human creation. As shadows, they can be dispelled by the Light of human beings; you should not fear them, for fear is their nourishment. But they are rooted in ancient habits and ways of being, and this gives them strength. If they can push you from your calm center and throw you off balance, they gain an advantage. You must be strong in your balance. This strength can be augmented by spiritual allies and the energies they link with yours, just as individuals who are linked arm in arm can be stronger and more stable than one person standing on his own. The easiest place for these energies of balance and connection to reach you as an incarnate being is through the subtle environment around you. As you have seen, you are empowered when you stand as part of the Commons.

The second reason is related. There are not only stressful and threatening energies set loose in the world. There are powerful energies of new creation. The Light of Gaia moves amongst you to inspire new ways of being. This Light is strong as well, stronger than a single person can embody. There is no single messiah or savior who will carry the burden and be the singular Lightbearer. Now, this task falls to humanity itself. Again, you are empowered to take up this Light of transformation by standing in connection with your world. The place where this connection is easiest to take place is with the allies present in your subtle environment.

It is for these two reasons that we have been emphasizing what is around you rather than that which is beyond you, elsewhere in the world.

Underlying both these reasons is a single foundation. It is the principle of partnership and collaboration. This is the key that will enable you to meet both the challenges and the opportunities of the days ahead. This is collaboration with others who share your incarnate state and collaboration with those of us in the subtle dimensions. Who is closer with whom you can practice this collaboration than the beings who are in your subtle environment? Join their communion, their Commons, and stand in the power of your partnership.

MARY: From my perspective, "local" and "planetary" can be misleading if you think of yourselves as being one or the other. You embody a wide range of attunement and connection. You have a planetary aspect as well as a local one. Do you think the high Angels and their Devic counterparts are unaware when you reach out to them? They rejoice at your desire to serve and to be a blessing to life wherever it may be suffering in the world. But they themselves are not solely "planetary" beings; they are rooted in the earth and in what you experience as the energies of your subtle environment. They can partner with you more fully and easily if you share this rootedness with them.

I can see in you and others the desire to help with your Light those at a distance suffering from the calamities that erupt in your world now. What you call subtle activism is a gift any of you can offer, and it is received with appreciation and love. But understand this from our perspective. Imagine if you had a patient who suffered from inflammation in their body. As a result, boils and sores would appear here and there, causing pain and discomfort. You want to treat the boils, for they are a source of irritation, but when you draw the poison out of one, another appears; when you heal one sore, two more erupt. The problem is not only with the boils; they are what appear on the surface of the body. The problem is with the inflammation.

We wish to treat the boils and we honor your help in doing so, but even more, we wish to cure the inflammation. This is done through the subtle field that all incarnate life shares, what you call the subtle environment. You are part of this right where you are. The more you attune to and bless the life around you, the more resistant the whole body of Gaia becomes to the forces of inflammation.

We are not asking you to ignore the world beyond your locality. Why would we? You are part of that world, and it needs the love and the Light you can bring to it. But it is the subtle environment of the world that is most affected by this inflammation extending from the collective energy field of humanity, and it is here that it can be treated. Here you can connect with the healthy energies that naturally flow through Gaia's environments at all levels and use them to transmute and cleanse that which is broken.

As an incarnate soul, you have the capacities that your soul brings

65

you, the power of your Self-Light, and you also have direct connection to the subtle environment. Not only is this a place to which you can send your Light and blessings, but it is also where you can find partners that can benefit from as well as heighten the strength and power of your spiritual presence in the world.

It is in your wholeness and integration as a physical individual, a subtle being, and as soul that you become Gaia, and for Gaia, there is no planetary and no local, only the presence of life to be held, cherished, and empowered.

REFLECTIONS

Over the past year, I've been feeling an increasing need to focus on our connections with the subtle life around us. Earlier this year, my Lorian colleague Jeremy Berg asked if I could update the material I wrote on Techno-Elementals for the fourth issue of this Journal, nearly seven years ago, to make a new book. At first, I doubted that I could do it as I was busy with a number of other writing projects that I would have to set aside if I took up Jeremy's request. It did not seem as important a topic to me then as others I was working on. However, I had a strong push from my own subtle colleagues to do it. When I asked why, they said, "It's important to heighten awareness of the life that surrounds you, not just in nature where you expect it but in the environment you have built and the things you have produced. Connecting with this life in blessing and partnership is increasingly important." As a consequence, I spent the next six months writing a new book on Techno-Elementals and the subtle life in the things around us.

Doing so made me more aware than ever of the potentials existing in the subtle environment on which we can draw and also of the need that exists for us to engage with this part of our world and the good we can do there. Mary spoke of the "inflammation" that exists in subtle environments of the world, an inflammation of distorted and broken energy that gives rise to pain, fear, anger, and hatred. So much of this has been buried in our collective unconscious and is now surfacing to be dealt with. It exists in the collective energy field of humanity, but that field impinges upon and manifests through the subtle environment. It's like a dark mist rising from swampy ground. There are many sources of Light and wholeness in the subtle environment that can dispel this mist like the sun dispelling ground fog. What is important to realize is that we are one of those sources—and in some ways, we are one of the most vital of these sources since humanity is the cause of much of this miasmic emergence. We are the ones most able to confront the consequences of generations of bad habits.

But there is more to this than just performing subtle activism or energy hygiene. It is the pressure to give birth to a way of being, what I think of as a Gaian consciousness or a Gaian way of being. This is what the Lorian idea of Gaianeering is all about; it includes such activities as subtle activism but goes beyond it. It is, as I said above, about being as well as about doing.

The challenges, both human and environmental, that are rising up to meet us will require resiliency and collaboration, a willingness to work together to achieve mutual benefit. No person, no group, no nation can solve these challenges on their own. They are systemic problems, and all parts of the world system must be engaged. But the ability to collaborate emerges from a largeness of mind and heart. It requires a "spacious human," a person able to expand in consciousness to embrace otherness and difference.

This, I believe, is the nature of the Gaian human seeking to manifest. Being a Gaianeer means saying, "I am not helpless in the world. I have a power to draw upon, the power of my being, my Self-Light, in collaboration with life." It's not so much that we can make a difference in the world as it is that we *are* a difference in the world. This matters. Out of our ability to blend our difference with that of others, possibilities take shape and potentials can manifest. Change can occur. The world can transform.

We all have an innate talent, as incarnate souls, to "Gaianeer," to be and to act in ways that bring love and vitality into the world and enable the sacredness and potentials of Gaia to emerge. We don't have to earn this talent. But like any talent, we do need to practice it.

It's a new skill. It's not the way we've been taught to view the world, or ourselves. We have older habits of thought to work through, not least of which is learning to see everything in the world around us as alive in its own way. Like all practices, it may not be easy, but the results are more than worthwhile.

The subtle environment of life provides us with an immediate and accessible area for practice. It is not the end all and be all, but it is a place to start, a place where, as Phillip said, we can gather and build our pile of kindling that can feed the flame of our Self-Light.

A MESSAGE FROM ONE OF DAVID SPANGLER'S NON-PHYSICAL (SUBTLE) COLLEAGUES JULY 2019

[The following is a message I received from one of my subtle colleagues at a time when tensions were running high in the world as various natural and social crises were escalating.]

"For the foreseeable future, humanity will inhabit a world of increasing challenge, both physically and in the realms of thought, emotion, and subtle energies. Just as the seas rise, so, too, are tides of negativity being drawn out of the depths of human karma, rising to be seen in the light of day where they can be transmuted. How much an individual may be impacted by these energies depends on his or her circumstances, but no one is spared. It is the condition of the world at this time.

"Think of it as a pandemic in which everyone is exposed to viruses of fear, anger, and conflict. Exposure, though, does not mean illness is inevitable. Anyone can be immune and anyone can be a source of healing for others. It depends on how they tend their own energy field and what they generate to contribute to the world around them.

"This is a virus that seeks to agitate and unsettle the energies within you and around you, making it harder for you to stand in your sovereignty and sacredness, harder for you to be calm and centered, harder for you to be loving and open, harder for you to be clear in your thinking and feeling. The temptation to use this agitation as a means to weaken and manipulate is strong, and there are those who will succumb to it. This can happen on a global scale and it can happen in the everyday lives of individuals and their personal relationships. Wherever and however it happens, it complicates the efforts of healing and transmutation and makes the pressure of negativity more intense.

"The situation is not without hope. Just as on a cloudy day, the sun is still present, even if unseen, so in your lives, a whole and healthy world is also all around you. The life of Gaia is strong and the Light circulates and flows through her into the world. Life has not forsaken you, but you must make an effort to see it.

"We urge all whom you may contact to use whatever techniques,

69

training, or inner skills they know and have cultivated to do two things. The first is to hold themselves in a place of peace and fiery hope, a place of love. You each have many allies, not least of which is your own soul, to help you do this if you only ask. Claim your sovereignty in Light.

"The second is to be a source of calm, of hope, of love, of positive vision and positive energies for others. By your very nature, you cannot help being generative and influencing the subtle environments around you. By your choices and your intentions, you can determine what kind of influence you are. Take one step in bringing blessing into your world, and a thousand angels will support you in the steps that follow.

"Act! Act! Act! You are not alone!"

(In a Challenging World)

TWO BLESSINGS

[Here are two blessings that I have found particularly helpful in centering myself within my own field of energy and in dealing with subtle energies in the places where I happen to be.]

Blessing of Body
I accept and bless my body without reservation.

I accept and bless the world of which my body is a part.

I accept and bless my soul that lives as my body and in my world and choose the wholeness that connects them.

From this wholeness, may Light and Love, Joy and Hope radiate to all the Earth.

Four Blessings
Bless this place in which I am, with honor and gratitude for its presence and its gift of space.

Bless myself, with honor and gratitude for the uniqueness of spirit, life, insight, and creativity which I bring to the world.

Bless others around me, seen and unseen, with honor and gratitude for the gifts we bring to each other, for the creativity and energy that can emerge from our collaboration.

Bless the activity I undertake in this place, that it may prosper and be a blessing to all my world.

71

STANDING ACTIVISM

When I feel beleaguered and under siege by subtle energies, emotions, and thoughts arising from events of conflict and violence in the world, I remember that I can choose my response. I can choose the quality and type of subtle energies that I will broadcast, for I am a generative source, not a passive sponge, fated to take in and absorb whatever the world throws at me.

Standing in my Sovereignty, my Self-Light, my love is what I call "standing activism." Unlike subtle activism, it is not responding to or focused upon a specific person or situation. Instead, it is a way of saying, "This is who I am as presence of wholeness, a generative source of love and of blessing." It is an affirmation of the sacredness of our incarnation and of our unique identity and personhood. It's about being present to Gaia as part of the Earth's community of life—and being present to oneself as something new emerging within humanity: a Gaian individual.

Standing activism is about showing up as a presence of wholeness and well-being in the world in partnership with Gaia. What this might look like for you depends on you and the circumstances of your life. Like subtle activism itself, there's no one way, one technique, of doing it. But here's an illustration of how I approach it. I think of it as a series of "standings".

- I stand in my Sovereignty and my honoring and blessing of my own unique incarnate individuality. I show up to myself.
- I stand in the self-light and presence of my subtle energy field and all its connections to the unseen realms of the earth. I show up to my subtle nature.
- I stand in the joy of my soul, open to the currents of joy that move through the earth, that I might be a focus of distribution for this joy in the world around me. I show up to joy.
- I stand in the midst of the life that permeates the Earth and is unfolding in all things, human and non-human, organic and inorganic, physical and non-physical. I stand in celebration of this life and in service to its unfoldment. I show up to life.

- I stand in the midst of the promise of humankind, the promise of our evolution into love, into harmony and partnership with Gaia, into wholeness. I stand in the knowledge that I am, in this place and at this time, this evolution in process. I am the manifestation of the coming-into-being of the Gaian Human.

- I show up to my environment, whether it is one built by human hands or one emerging from nature and the Earth. I am a presence that carries all the qualities, all the energies and power needed right now to bring or to draw forth wholeness from this place.

- In my heart, in my mind, and in my willingness and love, I say to the Earth—to Gaia—and to all beings serving this world, "Here I am. Here I stand in connection and partnership with the earth."

If you "stand" in this way as a daily practice, it sets up a rhythm that connects you to the flow and energy of life within Gaia. If, when you are feeling particularly impacted by what's going on in the world, when you may be feeling particularly hopeless, particularly dismayed, it will center you and bring you back into balance. Even more, if you intentionally hold within yourself the life-affirming energy of Gaia and the loving energies of your own sacred humanity, you augment and multiply these qualities in your subtle environment. Standing activism transforms into a "standing in blessing."

I cannot stress how important a practice like this is. Feel free to shape this practice in whatever way seems comfortable for you, that is unique for you, because it's a practice of the unique relationship that you have with the world. I'm just suggesting one way to go about it. It's important for you to find a way that works for you.

You will know when you find that way because it will feel powerful. You will feel powerful. You will feel connected. You will feel spacious. You will feel that you are part of the great unfoldment of Sacred Humanity in the world.

This is not a difficult practice. Standing activism, standing in blessing, standing in your generativity and Self-Light can be done simply and quickly. It can be done in silence. It can be done whether you're standing or sitting. It can be done anywhere, at any time. In so doing, you are a partner with the forces of Light throughout the cosmos, connecting their blessings with the fabric of your life and of Gaian life.

When this partnership becomes a daily practice, and more, a way of life, then we become a force for the transformation of our world.

CONTINUING THE JOURNEY

If you wish to continue exploring and learning about the resources you have within yourself to deal with the subtle impacts from the world around you, and just as importantly, how you can contribute to making a subtle energetic difference in the world, here are some further resources.

The following books all deal with subtle energy tending and elaborate upon and deepen the material in this anthology. They are available from Lorian Association's website (www.lorian.org).

Journey Into Fire
Facing The Future
Working with Subtle Energies
Techno-Elementals
World Work

Views from the Borderland, my journal of explorations of the subtle realms and their relationship to our daily lives, is also available. You may subscribe by going to Lorian's website (www.lorian.org).

Lorian also provides webinars and classes on Incarnational Spirituality, personal empowerment, and working with subtle energies. Information on these classes may be found at www.lorian.org.

A FINAL NOTE:

This anthology focuses on things I have written and on work and ideas emerging from Incarnational Spirituality. There are many people throughout the world, though, actively generating positive ideas and hopeful visions. Seek them out. The Internet certainly can bring darkness, hatred, and anger to us but it can also be a tool that puts us in touch with Light, with goodness, with striving and inspiration, with positive ideas and visions. People are generating hope all the time in the form of books, videos, blogs, websites, and other forms of information exchange, but you may have to make an effort to find it. Mainstream media tends to ignore these sources in favor of sensationalism and conflict to sell their content. Be discerning, but spread your informational net if you are feeling hopeless about the future or about humanity. The hope is there, waiting to be caught.

And never forget: you can be a source of that hope for others.

ABOUT THE PUBLISHER

Lorian Press LLC is located in Holland, Michigan, USA. It is a private, for profit business which publishes works approved by the Lorian Association. Current titles can be found on the Lorian website lorian.org or the Lorian Press LLC website lorianpress.com.

The Lorian Association is a not-for-profit educational organization. Its work is to help people bring the joy, healing, and blessing of their personal spirituality into their everyday lives. This spirituality unfolds out of their unique lives and relationships to Spirit, by whatever name or in whatever form that Spirit is recognized. The address is:

The Lorian Association
PO Box 1368
Issaquah, WA 98027

For more information, go to www.lorian.org

CPSIA information can be obtained
at www.ICGtesting.com
Printed in the USA
LVHW050031240919
631983LV00004B/682/P

9 781939 790309